Also Available From the American Academy of Pediatrics

ADHD: What Every Parent Needs to Know

Autism Spectrum Disorders: What Every Parent Needs to Know

Baby and Toddler Basics: Expert Answers to Parents' Top 150 Questions

Building Resilience in Children and Teens: Giving Kids Roots and Wings

Caring for Your Baby and Young Child: Birth to Age 5*

Dad to Dad: Parenting Like a Pro

Food Fights: Winning the Nutritional Challenges of Parenthood Armed
     With Insight, Humor, and a Bottle of Ketchup

Guide to Toilet Training*

My Child Is Sick! Expert Advice for Managing Common Illnesses and Injuries

Raising Kids to Thrive: Balancing Love With Expectations and Protection
     With Trust

Retro Baby: Cut Back on All the Gear and Boost Your Baby's Development
     With More Than 100 Time-tested Activities

Sports Success R_x! Your Child's Prescription for the Best Experience

The Big Book of Symptoms: A–Z Guide to Your Child's Health

The Picky Eater Project: 6 Weeks to Happier, Healthier Family Mealtimes

Waking Up Dry: A Guide to Help Children Overcome Bedwetting

**For additional parenting resources, visit the HealthyChildren bookstore at
shop.aap.org/for-parents.**

 healthychildren.org
Powered by pediatricians. Trusted by parents.
from the American Academy of Pediatrics

*This book is also available in Spanish.

Retro TODDLER

More Than 100 Old-School Activities to Boost Development

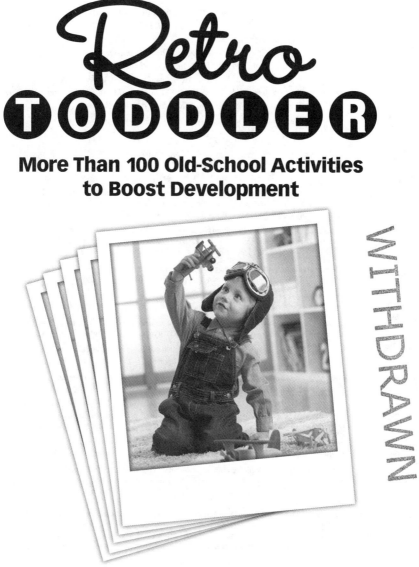

Anne H. Zachry, PhD, OTR/L

Pediatric Occupational Therapist
and Child Development Specialist

American Academy of Pediatrics

DEDICATED TO THE HEALTH OF ALL CHILDREN®

American Academy of Pediatrics Publishing Staff

Mark Grimes, *Vice President, Publishing*

Kathryn Sparks, *Manager, Consumer Publishing*

Holly Kaminski, *Editor, Consumer Publishing*

Shannan Martin, *Production Manager, Consumer Publications*

Linda Diamond, *Manager, Art Direction and Production*

Mary Lou White, *Chief Product and Services Officer/SVP, Membership, Marketing, and Publishing*

Sara Hoerdeman, *Marketing Manager, Consumer Products*

Published by the American Academy of Pediatrics
345 Park Blvd
Itasca, IL 60143
Telephone: 630/626-6000
Fax: 847/434-8000
www.aap.org

The American Academy of Pediatrics is an organization of 66,000 primary care pediatricians, pediatric medical subspecialists, and pediatric surgical specialists dedicated to the health, safety, and well-being of infants, children, adolescents, and young adults.

The information contained in this publication should not be used as a substitute for the medical care and advice of your pediatrician. There may be variations in treatment that your pediatrician may recommend based on individual facts and circumstances.

Statements and opinions expressed are those of the authors and not necessarily those of the American Academy of Pediatrics.

Listing of resources does not imply an endorsement by the American Academy of Pediatrics (AAP). The AAP is not responsible for the content of external resources. Information was current at the time of publication.

Products and Web sites are mentioned for informational purposes only and do not imply an endorsement by the American Academy of Pediatrics. Web site addresses are as current as possible but may change at any time.

Brand names are furnished for identification purposes only. No endorsement of the manufacturers or products mentioned is implied.

The publishers have made every effort to trace the copyright holders for borrowed materials. If they have inadvertently overlooked any, they will be pleased to make the necessary arrangements at the first opportunity.

This publication has been developed by the American Academy of Pediatrics. The contributors are expert authorities in the field of pediatrics. No commercial involvement of any kind has been solicited or accepted in development of the content of this publication. Disclosures: The author reports no disclosures.

Every effort is made to keep *Retro Toddler: More Than 100 Old-School Activities to Boost Development* consistent with the most recent advice and information available from the American Academy of Pediatrics.

Special discounts are available for bulk purchases of this publication. E-mail Special Sales at aapsales@aap.org for more information.

Printed in the United States of America
9-397   1 2 3 4 5 6 7 8 9 10
CB0104
ISBN: 978-1-61002-157-9
eBook: 978-1-61002-158-6
EPUB: 978-1-61002-159-3
Photography by Peri Jane Pate
Cover design by Peg Mulcahy

Library of Congress Control Number: 2017941934

What People Are Saying

Advance Praise for *Retro Toddler*

Anyone involved in childhood development will consider this book a resource to be treasured and referred to frequently. Dr Zachry has created a parent-friendly volume designed to connect research data with practical play activities that can provide an enhanced learning environment for toddlers. The breadth and scope of her book spans all areas of life skills, from gross and fine motor development to the emotional and behavioral facets of a child's learning. This book provides coverage of a number of important issues facing parents today, such as screen time, parenting styles, and early childhood literacy development. Every parent, childhood education teacher, and pediatric occupational therapist should have this book on their shelves.

Katherine J. Collmer, MEd, OTR/L
Author of *Handwriting Development Assessment and Remediation: A Practice Model for Occupational Therapists*

Retro Toddler provides the perfect balance of research-backed child development information and good old-fashioned "retro" activities to help parents resist the powerful and quite understandable lure of technology. Dr Anne Zachry's enthusiasm shines through each page as she shares occupational therapy and parenting tips that promote communication, social, and motor skills. However, even more importantly, readers will learn about the types of parenting style and play that help toddlers develop traits such as self-control, independence, and what the author describes as "grit." I highly encourage parents and others who work with and love children to read this wonderful sequel to *Retro Baby*.

Barbara A. Smith, MS, OTR/L
Author of *From Rattles to Writing: A Parent's Guide to Hand Skills* and *From Flapping to Function: A Parent's Guide to Autism and Hand Skills*

Praise for *Retro Baby*

This is a great book for any parent, but particularly for those who want to minimize the high-tech, often unnecessary, paraphernalia being pushed these days! Parents, you will appreciate the creative ideas for entertaining your baby and encouraging your baby's development.

Rachel Y. Moon, MD, FAAP
Professor of pediatrics, George Washington University School of Medicine and Health Sciences, Children's National Medical Center; editor in chief, *Sleep: What Every Parent Needs to Know;* chairperson, American Academy of Pediatrics Task Force on Sudden Infant Death Syndrome

It's great to see someone take notice of the wonderful way that experiences while awake in prone help the infant learn essential motor skills and do not require special expensive equipment. In addition, parents can be their child's first teachers of exploration, communication, social interaction, and sensory and manipulation skill using inexpensive toys. Many parents will learn that there are simple, easy ways to promote a baby's development.

Michael E. Msall, MD, FAAP, FAACPDM
Professor of pediatrics, University of Chicago Medicine Comer Children's Hospital, and cochair, Pathways.org Medical Round Table

Put down your smartphone and pick up this book. With plain-spoken, concise wisdom, Dr Zachry provides vital, research-backed information for parents of young children. Creative, interactive play with other children and adults supports healthy brain development in ways today's technology never will.

Retro Baby provides parents fun, money-saving activities that will set their children up for lifelong success.

Mark Bertin, MD, FAAP
Developmental pediatrician, author of *The Family ADHD Solution: A Scientific Approach to Maximizing Your Child's Attention and Minimizing Parental Stress,* and editorial advisor, Common Sense Media

To my children, Justin, Emily, and Hanna.
You have been my greatest teachers, and
I love you more than words can say.

Contents

Foreword

When my children were toddlers, here is how we would play: we'd go into the playroom, and they would start dumping out things that interested them. There would be blocks, puzzles, dolls, cars, little pots and pans, plastic vegetables, magic wands, balls, stacking cups—in retrospect, just way the heck too much stuff. I'd join them for a few minutes, then I'd start trying to put everything back where it belonged.

If Abby was playing with blocks, I had a moment to put the cars back in their bins. If she moved to cooking, I could tuck the dolls in their beds. I would pair little rubber bear cubs with slightly larger rubber mama bears, capes with wands, sorting shapes with shape sorters. Developmental pediatricians call this behavior *"parallel play."* Psychiatrists call it "obsessive-compulsive personality disorder."

As parents, we all want to give our children everything they need to succeed. The problem is that we often give them the wrong things. How else to explain how we ended up with not one but two "Old MacDonald" tractors, each with its own plastic barn animals, lights, and noises? Neither one got more than a few seconds' attention from the kids, but, darn it, I kept each one with its own farmer, cow, pig, and chicken right up until they went to Goodwill Industries or, as we called it, "the farm."

As a pediatrician and now a parent of teenagers, I have a message for you: don't make it so complicated. What toddlers need to build the skills to succeed in life are not tablets or apps or plastic barn animals that make sounds when you plug them into a battery-powered tractor. As you will see in this book, they need a little attention from you, along with a smattering of items that you'll mainly find in your household recycling bin.

My favorite thing about this book is how it reminds me that activities we adults find boring and mundane are exactly the sorts of tasks that can help toddlers build important developmental skills and have fun at the same time. Do you hate sorting laundry? Your toddler will delight in grouping items by color and type and naming everything she touches. Do you get bored in line at the grocery store? It's a perfect place to model self-regulation skills and to work on key concepts such as distraction. Is your toddler bored? Great! Don't try to fix it. That's when the mind is at its busiest coming up with creative ideas.

As you enjoy this book, you may find yourself remembering how to play again. You may end up hopping like a frog, walking like a crab, and crossing a floor of lava on pillow "rocks." Just remember, your kids are not on Pinterest. Most of the crafty ideas in this book are designed to go right back in the recycling bin whence they came. So grab a permanent marker, a toilet paper roll, and some discarded yogurt lids and milk jugs and get ready to really enjoy helping your toddler explore his world. You don't have to be an artist, an early childhood educator, or a physical therapist to give your toddler all the skills she needs to succeed in her world. You just have to be what you already are: a parent.

David L. Hill, MD, FAAP

Author, *Dad to Dad: Parenting Like a Pro*
(American Academy of Pediatrics [AAP], 2012)
Chair, AAP Council on Communications and Media

Acknowledgments

I would like to begin by thanking everyone at the American Academy of Pediatrics for their time, expertise, and commitment to this book. To Jeffrey Mahony and the team who worked on the cover, I appreciate your dedication and hard work. A big thank-you to the reviewers, Rebecca Baum, MD, Terri McFadden, MD, and Bonnie Kozial, and thank you to Dr David Hill for writing the foreword. Kathryn Sparks, I am especially grateful to you for encouraging me to write this book and for your valuable edits and recommendations.

I am deeply thankful for the support, encouragement, and love of Mike Zachry, my husband and best friend. I love and appreciate you more than you will ever know. Thanks to my children, Justin, Emily, and Hanna. You will always have my heart.

Finally, a special thank-you to my mother, Beth Wyatt, for your unwavering support and unconditional love. Your positive outlook and contagious laugh are a true source of inspiration to me and many others. You have always encouraged me to follow my dreams, and for that I am grateful.

Introduction

Navigating the toddler years is a challenge for many parents, and so often, there seem to be more questions than answers. Is it OK for my child to play games on a tablet? When will she be ready for toilet training? Should I let my toddler watch television? Are apps really educational? Why won't my child share his toys?

The toddler years can be both magical and challenging. During this period of rapid growth and development, your child is gaining experience with important life skills and gradually building a solid foundation for the future. Of course, there are troublesome behaviors that parents have to deal with, and figuring out how to address these behaviors can be extremely stressful.

Fortunately, this book shares research-based information and practical strategies that parents and other caregivers can use to help them deal with a variety of issues that are common during the toddler years, such as picky eating, toilet training, tantrums, hitting, and other difficult behaviors. Additionally, parents have to make decisions related to their child's technology exposure on a daily basis, and guidance is always helpful when making these important decisions. These pages can help steer parents when setting guidelines related to technology use and screen time exposure during the toddler years.

As a mother of three, author of the parenting book *Retro Baby,* and an occupational therapist who has worked in the pediatric field for more than 25 years, I understand the importance of limiting screen time and technology exposure, and I've seen firsthand how overuse of electronics can negatively affect child development. In fact, research suggests that excessive screen time and technology use can lead to obesity, poor sleep, attention problems, behavior issues, and poor performance in school. I also understand that active play is key for healthy child development. No doubt, it is one of the most important "occupations" of childhood. All young children need to engage in this occupation on a daily basis, because it fosters the development of language, social, emotional, and motor skills. Play also allows for opportunities for children to express feelings, make decisions, and use their imaginations, and once these skills are gained, they will last a lifetime!

This book

- Explains the development of problem-solving skills during the toddler years
- Includes a variety of unique activities to foster the development of empathy and social skills
- Details what is going on with language development between the ages of 1 year and 3 years
- Reviews the research on overexposure to screens during toddlerhood
- Explains the benefits of a back-to-the-basics parenting approach
- Includes a variety of engaging activities that enhance the development of *fine motor skills* and *gross motor skills*
- Shares a number of brain-boosting activities that your toddler will enjoy
- Describes how to make a variety of toys out of everyday household items that are age-appropriate and promote creativity

The information in this book will help you understand the crucial role you play in your toddler's development. By using this multifaceted resource, you will support your child's physical, mental, and social development while growing a special bond between the two of you.

What You'll Find in These Chapters

Chapter ❶ shares detailed information related to the development of cognitive, language, and social skills during the toddler years. It also stresses the importance of fostering brain development in a variety of ways.

Chapter ❷ provides an overview of research-based information related to the development of both *fine motor skills* and *gross motor skills* during the toddler years. It also includes a number of entertaining activities that are beneficial for motor skill development.

Chapter ❸ describes the impact that different parenting styles have on child development. This chapter will also address the scientific studies related to parenting young children, such as the best way to praise toddlers to set them up for success.

Chapter ❹ explains how toddlers need to participate in physically active play to gain important foundational skills. The text covers how engaging in playful activities helps prevent obesity and promotes health and wellness. The chapter also will explain the impact *pretend play* has on development.

Chapter ❺ provides a "parent-friendly" review of screen-time and digital media use as related to child development. The chapter covers current research on media and technology exposure and its effects on obesity, sleep, poor academic achievement, behavior concerns, and limited attention spans in children. It explains why it is critical to limit screen time, and it offers guidance (based on recommendations made by the American Academy of Pediatrics) on how technology can be appropriately used for educational purposes for your toddler.

Chapters ❻ through **❾** review the developmental stages of toddlerhood and include more than 100 old-school activities that promote the development of language and social skills. These engaging activities will also enhance your toddler's attention span, movement, balance, and both *gross motor skills* and *fine motor skills*. Instructions are provided for a number of developmentally stimulating toys that parents and toddlers can make together out of everyday household items.

To write clearly and without a sex bias, I will use "he" and "she" in alternating chapters.

A Solid Foundation

When toddlers spend time on electronic devices and gadgets, they are missing out on natural opportunities for learning. There is clear evidence indicating that overexposure to screen media negatively affects learning in the early years. Thank goodness, there are plenty of alternatives to technology use for young children, such as arts and crafts, games, and music. This book includes a variety of fun, low-tech, age-appropriate, developmentally stimulating alternative activities that your toddler will enjoy, with no electricity needed. It also offers guidance on how to deal with a variety of toddler-specific issues and how to promote your child's overall development the good old-fashioned way. Keep in mind that every child is unique and that it is important for parents to trust their instincts when dealing with their little ones, so be assured that there is no pressure to rigidly follow the recommendations in this book. Be flexible, keep an open mind, and adapt the provided suggestions as needed to meet your child's and your family's unique needs. As a mother of three, I know from personal experience that parenting can be a challenge at times, and it is my hope that the information in this book will help parents navigate the toddler years with confidence. These days, months, and years are going to fly by, so enjoy every moment and have fun making special memories with your child!

CHAPTER 1

The ABCs of Brain Development

The ABCs of Brain Development

Early experiences shape the structure and function of the brain.

~ Daniel Siegel

Have you ever wondered what is going on inside your toddler's mind? If so, keep reading. This chapter will explain your child's brain development during the toddler years so that you can better understand his behavior during this period of rapid growth. Knowing what to expect will be helpful as you navigate these foundational years.

The Developing Brain

Infants are born with approximately 100 billion brain cells, called "neurons," and during the early months and years after birth, these neurons send signals to each other. As the signals travel back and forth, connections are made and neural pathways are formed. This is how learning occurs. In fact, as the connections form and grow, your child is growing smarter. These pathways are basically the brain's wiring. The more often the pathways are used, the stronger the connections become, and strong connections are necessary for the development of language and motor skills, as well as behavioral and emotional development. No doubt, your child's experiences during the first years after birth directly affect the connectivity of these neural pathways.

Early brain development, also called "cognitive development," is influenced by a variety of factors, including genetics, sensory experiences, nutrition, physical activity, and relationships. Yes, families, friends, schools, and communities all have an impact on cognitive development during a child's early years. It is important to note that brain development doesn't happen all at once. The greatest brain growth occurs during the first 3 years after birth, and during these years there are prime periods when tasks or concepts are easily learned because so many connections are forming. Scientists call these optimal time frames for learning *critical* (or *sensitive*) *periods*. As you can see, these early years offer countless opportunities for a wealth of learning to occur.

Problem-solving Milestones in the Toddler Years

- **12 to 18 months:** Searches for an object hidden from view

- **18 to 24 months:** Turns an upside-down spoon right side up

- **24 to 30 months:** Pretends an object is something else

- **30 to 36 months:** Uses a chair to obtain an out-of-reach item

The brain is truly a spectacular organ! It has different sections, and each section is responsible for a particular job. For example, specific areas of the brain control language processing and speaking. The different areas of the brain are constantly working together to direct complex actions. Amazingly, the brain is very malleable. If one area of the brain is damaged because of a trauma or an illness, another area of the brain may take over for the damaged region. Isn't that miraculous? This is why it is so important to provide your child with sensory-rich experiences during the early months and years after birth.

Truth Be Told

Research suggests that a child's language abilities are related to his mother's vocabulary and literacy skills.[1]

How can you ensure that your child is learning and forming new brain pathways? Toddlers learn how the world works through their everyday experiences, so it is critical for parents to provide an abundance of opportunities for their little ones to explore their environment on a daily basis. When your child desires to see, touch, smell, and hear the world, allow him to do so in a safe manner. Encourage him to watch an airplane fly across the sky, touch a leaf on a tree, smell a fresh flower, and listen to a bird chirp. These simple, yet rich experiences are just what your developing child needs.

Being a loving and caring parent is another way to support early learning and nourish your child's brain growth. As we know, life can be extremely busy, but always remember that your child needs plenty of attention. It is important for him to know that you are there for him. So be intentional about finding time during your busy days to spend quality moments with your toddler. When your child has a need and you respond in a consistent manner, he feels safe and secure, allowing the two of you to build a deep emotional bond and a trusting relationship. No doubt, healthy infant-parent relationships provide a positive foundation for all of the child's future relationships.

During the toddler years, a child's *executive functioning* skills are beginning to develop. *Executive functions* are a group of mental skills that help an individual pay attention, plan, remember, and multitask. By using *executive functioning* skills, the brain tunes out distractions to remember information, think flexibly, and maintain *self-control*. This set of skills begins to develop in infancy and toddlerhood and does not mature until early adulthood. Research tells us that efficient *executive functioning* skills are important for learning and for future success in life. Strong relationships and opportunities to interact with others in infancy and early childhood provide a foundation for the development of *executive function* skills.[2] When parents model skills such as *self-control* and focus, they can be certain that children are watching and learning. A parent can also coach a child through difficult situations and tasks by providing just enough support to present an appropriate challenge while also ensuring that the child is successful. For example, if your toddler struggles to carry out tasks that involve multiple steps, such as brushing his teeth, you can prompt him during the task by asking, "Do you put the toothpaste on now?" As you can see, parents play an important role in supporting their child's brain development.

Brain-Boosting Activities

- Build a simple block structure and encourage your child to make a structure just like the one you made.

- Take 2 plastic cups and let your child watch you hide a small toy or object (large enough to not be a choking hazard) underneath one of the cups. Instruct him to watch carefully as you move the cups around each other, then ask him to select the cup with the toy under it.

- Provide nesting dolls for your child to nest and stack.

- While your toddler is looking in a mirror, ask him to point to various body parts, such as his nose, eyes, hair, and mouth.

Talk, Toddler, Talk!

The first 12 months after birth are important for speech and language development. For example, when a baby cries, blows bubbles, mouths his hand, and babbles, he is gaining skills that are foundational for speech. Around the age of 1, your little one will likely be able to speak several words, such as "Dada," "Mama," and "bye-bye." At this point, he understands much more than he can express. With time, he begins to put words together, and his ability to communicate expands. First come simple one-word requests, then phrases, and eventually full sentences. Keep your eyes and ears open, because it is so much fun to watch and hear your child gain new language every day.

When your child makes eye contact and speaks to you, you likely smile and verbally respond to him. With positive interactions such as this, you are promoting your child's language development. During this time of rapid development, your toddler should be exposed to as much language as possible, so talk to your child about everything he sees and hears. It is also important to talk to your toddler when you are engaged in daily routines if he is nearby. For example, if your child is in the room while you are folding laundry, say, "Look at this fluffy towel I am folding. It is yellow. It is yellow just like the school bus your sister rides to school. Can you say yellow?" Your little one will enjoy the communication, and his language skills will benefit from the interaction. Invite your child to assist with sorting and organizing the laundry. He will have fun dividing and putting all the socks and washcloths into piles. Labeling, such as "socks" or "towels" in this task, is another great way to build your child's vocabulary.

The Power of Nursery Rhymes and Songs

Nursery rhymes and songs teach young children about words and language. That's why this book includes a variety of traditional rhymes and songs that will strengthen your toddler's emerging language skills and grow his vocabulary. Enjoy reciting, reading, and singing the songs and nursery rhymes in the following chapters with your little one!

Baa, Baa, Black Sheep

Baa, baa, black sheep,
Have you any wool?
Yes, sir, yes, sir,
Three bags full;
One for the master,
And one for the dame,
And one for the little boy
Who lives down the lane.

When taking a walk around the house or neighborhood, point to different objects and have your child name each item. The more words he hears, the more his vocabulary will grow. By listening to others and communicating regularly, your child is gaining new words and improving his communication skills every day. Very soon, your toddler will be talking nonstop, so prepare yourself!

A toddler's frequent questioning can be overwhelming at times. I know this firsthand! When my children were toddlers, I remember receiving constant questioning: "What is that, Mommy? Why not, Mommy? Why?" As their communication skills improved, there were occasions on which I didn't even know the answers to their questions! The good news about all the questioning is that children are naturally compelled to learn. They are full of curiosity, and they want to gain as much information as possible about this great big amazing world.

If your toddler asks a question and you don't know the answer, think of it as the perfect teaching opportunity. Go to the library together and explore a variety of books in search of an answer. Make sure that the books include plenty of colorful pictures. It will be a special experience as your child becomes familiar with the library and the fascinating world of books. Shared times like this will have a lasting impact on your toddler and foster a true lifelong love of learning!

The Power of Regular Reading

When a parent reads regularly to a child, it helps him develop a love of reading. Research tells us that reading stimulates brain development and has a positive impact on social skills, language, and future reading ability.[3-5] No wonder the American Academy of Pediatrics recommends that parents regularly read aloud to their children beginning in infancy.

When reading to your toddler, use an animated voice, point to pictures, and encourage him to point to, name, and describe objects and characters. This will make the experience fun for both of you. Keep in mind that there are different kinds of books that will appeal to your child, including scratch-and-sniff, lift-a-flap, board, and tactile books. These types of books make the reading experience interactive and engaging.

A wonderful way to promote reading in your child is to visit your public library on a regular basis. The library is entertaining and offers a wealth of resources for both parents and toddlers. Interestingly, recent research reveals that parents who own a library card are more likely to read to their young children than are those who do not, and children whose parents have a library card have higher reading scores when tested.[6]

Emotion

The ability to communicate plays an important role in emotional and social skill development, and having strong language skills is important for success in school and in life. As your child matures and his vocabulary improves, you can help him learn how to recognize and label his emotions. For example, when he wants something that he can't have, say, "I can tell you are very frustrated right now." Every time you label an emotion that your toddler expresses, he will begin to associate that label with how he is feeling. Having words for specific emotions will help your toddler learn how to appropriately express himself when he's frustrated, angry, and excited.

Truth Be Told

Research reveals that empathy is positively associated with prosocial behaviors.[7] This means that individuals who are empathetic are likely to be kind and helpful to others.

As your toddler learns to manage his feelings, he is taking an important step toward gaining self-regulation skills. What is self-regulation? It is the capability of controlling one's impulses, observing and interpreting the reactions of others, managing feelings, and acting appropriately in social situations. For example, when your child is at a friend's birthday party, he is expected to sit nearby and observe as his friend opens gifts. Your toddler has to inhibit the urge to rush forward and unwrap the gifts himself. You can support your child by whispering to him that this is not his birthday party and these are not his presents, so it is not appropriate for him to open them. By doing this, you are helping your toddler develop self-regulation. Individuals who have strong self-regulation skills can socialize in a healthy manner and function better in life than those who are unable to self-regulate.

Early emotional and social experiences influence the development of *self-control,* so it is important for parents to provide a secure and nurturing environment during the early years. Parents also serve as role models by practicing *self-control* on a daily basis. Waiting until everyone is finished with dinner to have dessert and waiting patiently in line at the grocery store are examples of the role modeling of *self-control.* No doubt, self-regulation is an important life skill that we want our children to master!

The ability to self-regulate is associated with solid academic skills.[8]

Empathy

During these early years, your child is beginning to understand that he is a separate, individual person. He is also becoming attentive to the facial expressions and actions of others, and these abilities are critical for building and maintaining relationships. During the toddler years, there are countless opportunities for parents to teach their little ones about how other people think and feel, and this plays a key role in the development of empathy. When a child is empathetic, he is aware of the feelings of another person and is capable of taking that person's perspective. Empathy typically begins to develop in late toddlerhood, and it is the cornerstone of emotional and social development. For example, if you stub your toe and cry out in pain, your toddler may offer you his stuffed animal. It is likely that he understands that you are sad and are physically hurting, and he wants to make you happy. As a parent, it is also important to communicate with your child about empathy. For example, when reading books together, point out how a particular character feels in a situation or ask your child how the character might feel. This will help him understand others' emotions. Also, remember that you are your child's first teacher, and by being empathetic toward others, you are teaching him how to do the same.

Truth Be Told

Children who grow up with a pet display more empathy than those who do not.[9]

Making Friends

As your toddler is learning to empathize, he is also learning how to socialize appropriately. He is gaining necessary social skills such as the ability to follow rules, patiently wait his turn, behave in a safe and appropriate manner, share and play well with others, and control his impulses. Spending time with peers provides opportunities for your child to practice social skills. This socializing can take place during playdates or at child care. Gaining these skills is important for forming friendships in the future. When a child develops strong social skills, he is more apt to be well-liked by his peers and engage in positive interactions with playmates.

Jack and Jill

Jack and Jill went up the hill
To fetch a pail of water.
Jack fell down and broke his crown,
And Jill came tumbling after.

Up Jack got, and home did trot,
As fast as he could caper.
He went to bed to mend his head,
With vinegar and brown paper.

Learning From His Mistakes

It is so difficult to allow our children to fail. Parents never want to see their children discouraged or struggling. This can be painful to watch, especially when we know that we have the ability to step in and make everything OK. Yet, every child needs to experience failure and persevere, even a toddler! Learning how to face and overcome struggles and obstacles builds character and confidence and helps with the development of problem-solving skills. If you jump in and handle every challenging situation for your child, you are increasing the need for reliance and preventing opportunities for growth. Instead, give your child plenty of room, ask questions, and provide subtle suggestions that will help your toddler solve problems independently. For example, if he is working a puzzle and has difficulty finding the correct piece, don't rush in and point out the one he needs. Instead, give him a choice: "Do you think this piece fits there, or is it this one?" When he successfully completes the puzzle, not only will your toddler be proud of his accomplishment, he will gain confidence. Soon you will hear him saying, "I can do it all by myself!" And that will be music to your ears.

Truth Be Told

To develop problem-solving skills, toddlers need to be adaptable, curious, and persistent.[10]

As you have learned in this chapter, the toddler years are a period of rapid growth and development. The brain is constantly forming new connections, and your little one is beginning to develop a sense of self. Language skills are exploding, and your toddler is gaining social skills that will enable him to eventually make and keep friends. During this *critical period,* the bond between you and your child will solidify, allowing him to feel safe and secure. The attachment that the two of you share empowers your child to venture out and explore the world. Of course, now you know that this is how learning occurs!

CHAPTER 2

Early Movement Matters

CHAPTER 2

Early Movement Matters

Your children need your presence more than your presents.

~ Jesse Jackson

Toddlerhood is a fascinating time in your child's life. As she explores the world around her, she is constantly learning about her surroundings and herself. Her developing motor skills enable her to control her actions so that she can investigate every new object and location that piques her curiosity. As she interacts with the world physically, her motor skills are improving. This chapter provides an overview of motor skill development and shares a number of simple yet fun activities that promote the development of *gross motor skills* and *fine motor skills*. Having a basic understanding of motor skill milestones will be helpful when selecting toys and play activities for your child.

A Solid Foundation

When a baby is born, involuntary physical reflexes primarily direct her movement. This means that she has limited control over the muscles in her body. Slowly but surely, as time passes, an infant gains the ability to move and direct her body in a coordinated manner. First, she gains the strength to hold her head in an upright position, and then she begins to turn it from side to side. Before you know it, she is rolling over, sitting up, crawling, and walking!

Gross Motor Milestones

- **12 months:** Pulls to a standing position

- **18 months:** Can run, although falls easily

- **24 months:** Kicks a large ball

- **30 months:** Jumps with both feet off the ground

- **36 months:** Balances on one foot for several seconds

Tummy time play, rolling over, and the ability to sit upright are all actions that strengthen a child's neck, trunk, and shoulder muscles. These muscles form the base of postural control, also known as "core strength." Core strength provides a foundation for the more complex movements that a child eventually masters, such as sitting with upright posture, bringing hands together for play, and manipulating small objects. If a baby does not spend enough time playing on her stomach and rolling around during the first months after birth, she may not gain adequate strength in the neck, shoulders, and trunk to provide a solid platform for the mastery of the more refined motor skills that are so important during the school years. If your toddler resisted tummy time as an infant and you suspect that she has weakness in her core muscles, carry out several of these activities 2 or 3 times per week to strengthen those muscles. When you notice that your toddler is sitting upright more easily and frequently, it is a sign that the exercises are working. To continue strengthening your toddler's core muscles, feel free to gradually make the activities more challenging by having her wheelbarrow-walk further or hold the airplane pose just a bit longer.

Activities to Improve Core Strength and Gross Motor Skills

Activity 1: Wheelbarrow Walking

Help your child to lie on her stomach. Show her how to push up with her hands as you hold her by the knees so that she is in a push-up position. Encourage her to take several "steps" forward by walking with her hands. You may need to demonstrate this ahead of time. A fun way to motivate her to move forward is to place a favorite stuffed animal 3 or 4 feet in front of her.

Activity 2: Let's All Crawl

Play interactive games that involve crawling on the hands and knees. Devise races to retrieve a toy across the room, or construct an obstacle course out of sofa cushions and pillows for your little one to crawl through. For an adventure, get on your hands and knees and join your toddler in the fun!

Activity 3: Fly Like an Airplane

Show your toddler how to lie on her stomach on a soft, flat surface and lift her head, arms, and legs as if she is "flying like an airplane." Encourage her to hold the position as she "flies" to different places. Participate in the activity alongside your child and strengthen your core as well!

Activity 4: Rock the Boat

On a carpeted floor, position yourself on your back with your knees bent and your arms wrapped snugly around your shins. Slowly rock your body back and forth and encourage your toddler to imitate what you are doing. She may need your assistance to get her body into the position, so be prepared to help her. Once she has the hang of it, sing a song while she rocks back and forth. Switch from a song with a slow beat to one with a fast beat and encourage her to rock to the rhythm.

Activity 5: Having a Ball

Hold your toddler at her hips while she's positioned on her stomach over an ottoman or firm pillow and instruct her to toss a ball at an empty container. This is beneficial for core strength, and it also strengthens the shoulder and arm muscles.

On the Go!

Your toddler has places to go and people to see, and her developing *gross motor skills* will allow her to do just that! (*Gross motor skills* are the ability to control the large muscle groups of the body that are used during activities such as standing, walking, jumping, and climbing.) As discussed earlier, a strong core provides a solid base for future motor skills, and the core muscles are also critical for balance. During the toddler years, it is important for your child to have plenty of opportunities to be active and experiment with her motor skills so that she can strengthen the larger muscles. Active play in open spaces is extremely important for the development of *gross motor skills,* so limit the amount of clutter in your home and yard whenever possible.

As your child's *gross motor skills* mature, she will begin to climb to get to out-of-reach items. A basic child-sized stool can be helpful in promoting independence, especially if your child needs to reach the sink to wash her hands, retrieve clothing from a top drawer, or reach a favorite book on the top of her bookshelf. Keep all potential poisons, such as medicines, cosmetics, and cleaning products, as well as small or breakable items out of sight and reach of your child. All tall furniture—dressers and bookshelves in particular—MUST be secured to the wall with straps or screws.

It's so much fun to watch as your toddler masters the ability to walk, run, and climb. Once a child begins to walk independently, she is typically in nonstop motion!

Keep a close eye on her at all times, because her motor coordination isn't fully developed, so bumps and falls will likely be a frequent occurrence. As an early walker, she will be curious and full of excitement and motivated to explore her surroundings, but her safety awareness will be limited, so be on the alert for the occasional boo-boo. All tall furniture—dressers and bookshelves in particular—MUST be secured to the wall with straps or screws. Televisions should be mounted to the wall, screwed down to a sturdy stand that is designed to hold TVs, or strapped to the wall. Anchoring hardware can be purchased at baby or hardware stores at a low cost. Once your toddler gains control of her body and her balance improves, she will have more stability, and there will be fewer bumps and bruises. As her coordination and agility improve, she will navigate about with more ease. Thankfully, by the age of 3, she will have mastered the ability to catch herself when she falls.

Truth Be Told

As your child's motor skills develop, she has more opportunities to explore her surroundings and interact with others, which affects the development of her language skills.[11]

Opportunities to Be Active (Parents, too!)

Unfortunately, research reveals that many children younger than 5 years are not as physically active as they should be.[12] How can parents encourage their young children to be physically active? One of the best ways is for Mom and Dad to get active! Consider taking a long walk together, going to a parent-child exercise class, or playing tag with your child. Research tells us that a child's activity level is directly linked to how active her parents are.[13] So, whenever possible, find the energy to get moving. Remember, your toddler is watching!

Another benefit to being active is that it decreases the risk of obesity. The more physically active your child is early in life, the greater the likelihood that she will be physically active when older, thus decreasing her risk of being overweight. Make sure that your toddler has plenty of opportunities to run, climb, and explore while under your watchful eye. This will increase the likelihood of her staying healthy and fit into adulthood. Here are several activities that will keep your child on the move!

Activities to Promote Movement and Develop Coordination

Activity 1: Bottle Bowling

Use six to eight 16-ounce clean, empty plastic milk bottles. Find a clear space and arrange them as if they were bowling pins. Show your little one how to roll a large beach ball to knock them over. To make the game more challenging, use a smaller ball.

Activity 2: Feely Feet

Make a textured "obstacle course" for your child to walk on, using different fabrics and other materials. As she steps on the various textures, ask her to tell you how each one of them feels. This is a wonderful way for her to experience sensory feedback through her feet during movement.

Activity 3: On the Road Again

Draw a simple neighborhood with several roads and houses on a poster board or large piece of butcher paper and tape it to the floor. Show your child how to push a toy car on the roads while in a hands-and-knees position. Include stop signs and parking places so that she can learn when to stop and go and how to park her car.

Activity 4: Mommy Says

We are all familiar with the game of "Simon Says." "Mommy Says" is an amusing take on that popular children's game. Here are some fun directives to include when playing this game with your toddler: "Mommy says flap your wings like a bird. Mommy says walk like an elephant. Mommy says act like a monkey. Hop on one foot." If your child hops on one foot, remind her that you didn't start with "Mommy says," so it's time to start the game over! (You can also alter this game to be "Daddy Says" or "Grandma/Grandpa Says.")

The Mulberry Bush

Here we go 'round the mulberry bush,
The mulberry bush, the mulberry bush,
Here we go 'round the mulberry bush
So early in the morning.

This is the way we wash our face,
Wash our face, wash our face,
This is the way we wash our face
So early in the morning.

This is the way we comb our hair,
Comb our hair, comb our hair,
This is the way we comb our hair
So early in the morning.

This is the way we brush our teeth,
Brush our teeth, brush our teeth,
This is the way we brush our teeth
So early in the morning.

This is the way we put on our clothes,
Put on our clothes, put on our clothes,
This is the way we put on our clothes
So early in the morning.

Fine Motor Skills

Your toddler's gross motor abilities develop before her *fine motor skills* do. *Fine motor skills* are the ability to coordinate the hands and fingers when manipulating small objects. *Fine motor skills* and vision work together to coordinate movement, and eye-hand coordination is important in daily living skills such as feeding and dressing, which in turn lead up to more advanced tasks such as writing and cutting.

When your child was a baby, you may remember her arm and hand control began with reaching, swiping, and batting at desired items. Your child likely first grasped a small toy by closing her fingers around it and pressing the item against the palm of her hand. During early hand development, a baby moves all the fingers at once, but isolated finger movements soon follow!

Truth Be Told

Research demonstrates that there is a connection between *fine motor skill* development and future science, math, and reading skills.[14] In a 2010 study, investigators wanted to know which developing skills in early childhood predicted later math and reading achievement. They discovered that attention, general-knowledge test scores, and *fine motor skills* all together were strong predictors of subsequent math, reading, and science achievement.[14]

By the time your little one is 12 months of age, she will be using the tips of her thumb and index finger to pick up small objects. This is called a *pincer grasp,* and it is one of the first *fine motor skills* a baby masters. As your toddler touches, holds, and manipulates various objects with her hands, she takes in sensory information that helps her learn about the physical characteristics of the items she is manipulating. These experiences play a key role in hand skill development.

When your toddler is around 15 months of age, she will begin to develop more refined manipulation skills. For example, she will learn how to pick up cereal and bring them from her fingertips into her palm. (She will also be able to pick up small objects that may be choking hazards, so watch out!) By 24 to 30 months, she will begin to bring cereal from her palm out to her fingertips one at a time. By the age of 24 months, your child should be able to hold a crayon in a fisted position and color by using whole-arm movement. She will also be learning how to use both hands together in a coordinated manner, such as pulling pop beads apart and snapping them together. These movements are precursors to the more advanced hand skills that are needed for future school tasks. As your little one spends more time exploring familiar items, she will repeat certain movements, developing what therapists call "muscle memory." As her muscle memories increase, her *fine motor skills* continue to improve, and she will eventually gain the ability to feed and dress herself, which are key skills for developing independence.

Activities of Daily Living

Feeding and dressing skills are often called *activities of daily living* (ADLs) by medical professionals, such as pediatricians and therapists. Between the ages of 12 and 36 months, your toddler will make great strides in gaining independence with her ADLs. Around the ages of 12 and 18 months, you will notice that she is beginning to take an interest in dressing, and she may even try to undress on her own. She'll begin to take her socks and shoes off, even when you don't want her to! She may also provide some assistance with dressing. For example, she will likely hold her arms out and push them through sleeves when you are helping her put on shirts, sweaters, and coats.

John Jacob Jingleheimer Schmidt

John Jacob Jingleheimer Schmidt—

His name is my name, too!

Whenever we go out,

The people always shout,

"There goes John Jacob

Jingleheimer Schmidt!"

Da da da da da da da...

Truth Be Told

A recent research study revealed that preschoolers who had good visual-motor skills at the start of the school year scored higher with their *executive function* skills at the end of the year than did children whose visual-motor skills were not as strong. In the same study, the researchers found that children with better manipulative skills in the fall demonstrated more cooperative behaviors and better social skills the following spring.[15]

Your toddler will begin to use a spoon to scoop and eat at around 18 months of age, and she will likely start using a fork by 30 months. At around 24 to 30 months of age, your child may attempt to assist with simple fasteners during dressing. Encourage her to unbutton large buttons and unsnap jackets or sweaters. Allow for extra time when dressing so that she doesn't feel any pressure, and be sure to provide assistance as needed so that she will be successful with these tasks. She will be proud of her accomplishments, and so will you!

Fine Motor Milestones

Every child develops at her own rate, so keep in mind that the mastery of milestones varies from one child to another.

- **12 months:** Places large objects into a container

- **18 months:** Stacks 2 blocks

- **24 months:** Removes socks, coat, and hat

- **30 months:** Strings large beads

- **36 months:** Works a 3- to 4-piece puzzle

It may be difficult to imagine now, but time will pass quickly, and it won't be too long before your child is approaching school age. Obviously, *fine motor skills* are extremely important for school readiness. As we know, children use *fine motor skills* throughout the day once they start school, yet *fine motor skills* are not typically taught in school. That means that exposing your toddler to fine motor practice activities will increase her chances of eventually being successful in the classroom. Gaining strength and *dexterity* along with controlling and directing basic movements during the toddler years helps children build a solid foundation for future skills, such as holding a pencil correctly, writing, drawing, and cutting with child-safe scissors. The following activities will promote the development of *fine motor skills*. Keep play safe by closely supervising your toddler when she is carrying out these tasks.

Activities to Improve Fine Motor Skills

Activity 1: Pinch and Place
Squeezing clothespins and placing them on the edge of a small box or container is a wonderful way to strengthen the tiny muscles in your child's hands. This is also a great activity to promote eye-hand coordination and *dexterity*. Take several small pieces of colorful duct tape, wrap each piece around a clothespin's end, and place a strip of each color of tape on the edge of the container. Now you have a fun color-matching game that your child will enjoy.

Activity 2: Finger Painting Play
Tape a big piece of butcher paper to an outside wall in a garage or on a deck. Have your child use her index finger to imitate and copy basic lines and shapes with finger paint.

Activity 3: Spray Away!
Fill a small spray bottle with water and encourage your child to help you clean surfaces such as the kitchen table. The action of squeezing the trigger will strengthen the muscles in your child's index finger.

Activity 4: Popping Fun

Show your toddler how to pop bubble wrapping used for packaging. This is a good way to strengthen the thumb and index finger, and it's also fun to hear the *pop, pop, pop!* The sound will surely bring a smile to your child's face and maybe even elicit a giggle.

Activity 5: You Can't Go Wrong With Tongs

Another unique way to address *fine motor skills* is to have your child play with a set of child-sized tongs. These are typically available in educational and therapy stores, and there are a variety of ways to play with tongs that your toddler will enjoy. Opening and closing the tongs strengthens the tiny muscles in the hands and improves *dexterity*. Have your child use the tongs to place small blocks into various containers. Encourage her to count the blocks as she picks them up and places them on top of each other as quickly as possible. She will learn about numbers while also gaining strength and coordination in her hands.

Activity 6: Dress for Success!

Playing dress up is an opportunity for your child to gain arm and hand control. Provide her with a variety of hats, colorful clothing, and fun accessories. Visit your local thrift store and shop for several inexpensive outfits. Make sure that the clothing pieces have buttons, snaps, or zippers that are securely fastened and no drawstrings or decorations that could be pulled off. Start with large fasteners and, once your child masters those, progress to smaller ones. Playing dress up encourages *pretend play*, which is wonderful for your child's imagination.

Activity 7: Play-Doh Play

Manipulating Play-Doh is excellent for refining *fine motor skills*. Have your child form balls using only the thumb, index, and middle fingers of one hand, making the balls as smooth as possible. It is also fun to roll the clay into a long snake. Once the snake is complete, show your toddler how to pinch the body of the snake from the head all the way to the tip of the tail. This will be beneficial for her *pincer grasp*. (Make sure to keep a watchful eye on your child so she does not put any Play-Doh in her mouth.)

Activity 8: Tearing It Up!

Believe it or not, tearing paper into small pieces is a good activity that strengthens the small muscles in your child's hands. It also gives her practice using her 2 hands together. Have her tear several different types of colorful paper, such as construction paper, tissue paper, and index cards. With your help, she can glue the paper pieces to a larger piece of card stock to make her very own artistic masterpiece! Be sure to display her artwork to show her how proud you are of her hard work.

Activity 9: Up-and-Down Game

Show your toddler how to stand while holding onto a low surface, such as the edge of a sofa. Place several favorite toys on the floor and encourage her to squat down and retrieve one of the toys. Have her return to standing and place the toy on the couch. Tell her that she's going up and down "like an elevator." Encourage her to repeat the process until she has retrieved all the toys and put them on top of the sofa. This is a nice activity to address your toddler's leg strength and balance.

Activity 10: Just My Size

A child-sized desk or table and chairs are nice to have when your toddler is engaged in fine motor play. When seated, your child's feet should be flat on the floor with her elbows at or slightly above the level of the table or desktop. If she's positioned well, she will have more stability, allowing her to focus on the task at hand, such as coloring, and to use her arms and hands more efficiently.

> **Truth Be Told**
>
> A 2012 research study found that children who were advanced in their *fine motor skills,* particularly the ability to copy shapes and designs, had stronger literacy and comprehension scores compared with children who had less developed *fine motor skills.*[16]

Don't feel pressured to purchase a lot of expensive toys to promote your toddler's *fine motor skill* and *gross motor skill* development. It is not necessary to spend your hard-earned money on toys that light up, flash, blink, and make sounds. Remember, back to the basics is the key. No batteries are needed! A variety of simple toys will do. Keep in mind that your child shouldn't be overwhelmed with too many choices. If you find that her play space is cluttered with too much "stuff," pack some of the toys away for a month or so and rotate them back out later. She will be excited after the rotation. It will be just like having new toys!

As you have learned in this chapter, there are a variety of activities your child will enjoy that are beneficial for her motor skills. Encourage your toddler to engage in these entertaining activities, but don't be rigid or try to force her to participate. Remember, playtime should be relaxed and fun. You will enjoy watching firsthand as your toddler becomes more and more familiar with her body and masters the motor skills discussed in this chapter.

CHAPTER 3

Parenting Your Toddler: Why "Back to the Basics" Is Best

CHAPTER 3

Parenting Your Toddler: Why "Back to the Basics" Is Best

Imagination is more important than knowledge.

~ Albert Einstein

Have you ever heard the term *parenting style?* This term refers to the approach that parents use when raising their child, such the type of discipline used and the degree of responsiveness to the child's needs. In this chapter, I will describe the different types of parenting styles and review research related to parenting, including studies on *self-control, mindset,* and *grit.* I will also share practical strategies that parents can implement to set toddlers up for success, such as the best way to praise. Your sweet child is transforming into a little person, and it is important to consistently build his confidence by taking advantage of opportunities to praise him. As you will learn in this chapter, the way you praise your toddler has the potential to shape his outlook as he grows older.

Parenting Styles

There is solid research telling us that parenting style influences the kind of relationship you have with your child. Your particular parenting style also affects your child's development in a variety of ways. There are four main parenting styles: *authoritative, permissive, authoritarian,* and *uninvolved.* When caring for your child, you may use only one style, or you may combine particular aspects of the different styles. As you continue reading, consider which parenting style best describes your approach.

A *permissive* parent is highly responsive and indulgent. Children with *permissive* parents tend to get what they want when they want it. Parents who use this approach avoid conflict and confrontation whenever possible, doing whatever is necessary to avoid a tantrum. The structure is limited, and there are very few rules in the home, so, as you can imagine, a child raised with this approach rarely hears the word "no." The primary goal of a *permissive* parent is for the child to be happy. Expectations are low, leniency is high, few boundaries are set, and discipline is rare. Children whose parents are *permissive* tend to grow up to have limited *self-control* and engage in more maladaptive behaviors.[17,18]

On the other end of the spectrum is the *authoritarian parenting style*. A parent who uses this style is rigid and controlling, often saying "no" just for the sake of saying "no." An *authoritarian* parent sets firm rules and expects those rules to be followed without discussion or question. With this style, the parent is the strict authority, and the child must always be obedient. The commonly heard phrase "spare the rod, spoil the child" is consistent with this approach, meaning punishment and spanking are generally acceptable. Often, *authoritarian* parents demonstrate limited affection toward their children. When children are raised by *authoritarian* parents, they tend to have low self-esteem and poor social skills and are at increased risk of experiencing depression.[18,19]

American Academy of Pediatrics Policy on Spanking and Physical Discipline

"The AAP recommends a three-step approach toward effective child discipline. First, establish a positive, supporting and loving relationship with your child. Without this foundation, your child has no reason, other than fear, to demonstrate good behavior. Second, use positive reinforcement to increase the behavior you want from your child. Third, if you feel discipline is necessary, the AAP recommends that you do not spank or use other physical punishments. That only teaches aggressive behavior, and becomes ineffective if used often. Instead, use appropriate time outs for young children. Discipline older children by temporarily removing favorite privileges, such as sports activities or playing with friends. If you have questions about disciplining your children, talk with your pediatrician."[20]

Children raised by *permissive* parents are more likely to have poor *self-control.*[18]

The *authoritative parenting style* (also referred to as the "balanced" parenting style) is the middle ground between the *permissive* and *authoritarian* styles. This healthy approach to parenting commonly leads to a positive relationship between a parent and a child. Parents who embrace this style are supportive and have realistic expectations for their little one. They are also responsive to the child's emotional needs while setting clear and consistent limits. Children parented via the *authoritative* style tend to grow up to be well adjusted. They are also more likely to be committed to their school work, have a lower risk of depression, and demonstrate more life satisfaction than do children whose parents are *permissive* or *authoritarian.*[18,19,21]

Finally, there is the *uninvolved* or *disengaged* parenting style. With this style, parents tend to be less responsive, be more demanding, and offer limited support or encouragement. This results in a lack of closeness within the parent-child relationship. Children raised with this approach have an increased risk of eventually engaging in problem behaviors.[22]

If you currently use a *permissive, authoritarian,* or *disengaged* style and you are concerned about the possible negative outcomes, don't be distressed! It's never too late to make adjustments to your parenting style. The *authoritative* style is the most balanced, and because this approach leads to individuals who are confident, well adjusted, and emotionally healthy, this is the approach to strive for. Yet, there may be times when it's necessary to combine approaches for the best results. You may be wondering how a parent goes about adjusting his or her parenting style. If so, continue reading!

> **Truth Be Told**
>
> When mothers use a *permissive* parenting approach and fathers use an *authoritarian* approach, toddlers are more likely to engage in challenging behaviors.[22]

Adjusting Parenting Styles

During a parenting style transition, it's important to carefully consider your child's personality and temperament and do your best to address your child's specific needs. Children are all very different. One child might be very passive and content with the adjustment, while a change may rock another child's world. Pay close attention to how your toddler responds to any changes that you make, and gradually make adjustments in your approach as needed. For example, focus on being nurturing and responsive, while also providing clear expectations and boundaries. By being consistent and available while setting limits and actively listening to your toddler, you will be cultivating your child's resilience and *self-control.*

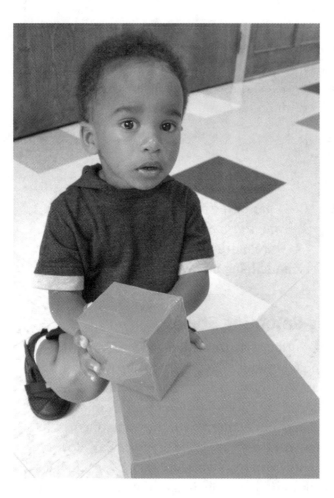

Mindset

We all have beliefs about learning and intelligence. Many individuals consider intelligence, ability, and character to be set at birth. In other words, they believe the traits with which you are born are what you have to work with throughout life, and these do not change no matter what. Researchers call this set of beliefs a *fixed mindset*. A contrasting outlook is the *growth mindset*. Individuals holding this stance believe that intelligence is malleable. They accept that hard work and effort have the potential to make a person smarter. Individuals who embrace a *growth mindset* are typically invested in learning and personal growth. Fortunately, as a parent, you can influence the mindset that your child develops, and one way to do that is through praise.

Praise

As parents, we are always excited when our child does something well. Whether he completes a task successfully, uses nice manners, or follows directions the first time, these are prime opportunities for praise. What many parents may not know is that *how* you praise your child matters. You may be thinking, "So there is a right way and a wrong way to praise a child?" Yes! Believe it or not, how we praise our children has been found to influence the type of mindset that our little ones eventually hold.

Has your toddler ever shown you something he made, and you briefly glanced over and said, "That's nice"? Of course, as busy parents, we are all guilty of this. Yet, it's likely that your child realized you weren't paying close attention. Remember, toddlers are taking it all in! So we should do our best to pause, attend closely, and provide a meaningful response. It is also important to be specific with our compliments by praising the particular behavior, action, or item as appropriate. For example, one might say, "Wow, I really like how you sat still, used your quiet voice, and colored your picture while we were in the waiting room today." Sharing specific details in this way helps a child understand exactly what was done well, and this will guide his behavior in the future. It will also boost his confidence!

Praise for Effort, Not Intelligence

When my children were young and they completed a task successfully, I used to say, "You are so smart! Well done!" What I didn't realize at the time was that the way I was praising them might have been doing more harm than good. Why? Studies suggest that not all praise is beneficial to children. The researchers assert that it is important to praise for effort and not smartness. In fact, the research reveals that *how* parents praise toddlers impacts a child's future motivation, self-esteem, and willingness to take on challenges.[23]

In one of the studies, the researchers videotaped inter-actions between mothers and their toddlers. The young children ranged in age from 1 to 3 years. During the study, the researchers carefully documented and tallied the type of praise that the mothers bestowed on their children. Some of the praise was directed at the child's effort, and some was directed at the child's talent or intelligence. For instance, a mother would say, "Good job building that tower out of blocks," and another mom might say, "Wow, you are a good builder." Five years later, when the children were school-aged, the researchers met with them to determine their mindsets. As the researchers hypothesized, the children who had been primarily praised for their effort as toddlers were more likely to take on challenging tasks as they grew older, and they were more likely to believe that hard work leads to improved performance.[23]

These findings suggest that as a parent, you play an important role in the particular mindset your child develops. Additional research confirms that the language used when communicating with a child also influences mindset. For example, in one study, a group of students with similar cognitive abilities was given a test. The children were divided into 2 groups; after testing, the first group was told, "Great job. You must be very smart," and the second group was told, "Great job. You must have worked very hard." Later, the students were given the opportunity to take another test. They were given the choice of 2 tests: one that they were told would be challenging and educational and another that would be easy. (The tests were identical.) A significant number of the children who were praised for being smart selected the easy task; most of the students praised for effort selected the challenging, educational task. The researchers concluded that praising the students for hard work led that group to want to learn new things, whereas praising children for intelligence led them to want to appear smart.[24]

Sticker Fun!

Kids love stickers. When a child pinches a sticker and peels it off a surface, this develops his *dexterity,* but that's not the only skill that can be addressed with stickers. You can use them to teach your toddler how to follow simple directions. Browse through a magazine together and instruct your child to peel a sticker off and place it on a specific item on the page—for example, "Put a sticker on the dog's face," or "Put a sticker on the dog's tail." Laugh together at how silly the dog looks! As your child gains skills, you can also work on directional concepts with him. Tell him, "Put a sticker under the car, on top of the car, or beside the car." Be sure to praise him for working hard!

Finally, in a third phase of the study, the same children were asked to complete a test that was similar to the first one they had taken. The children praised for effort performed significantly better on the follow-up test than did the children praised for intellect. The children praised for effort even reported that the test was fun; the children praised for intellect reported that the test was frustrating. Interestingly, the scores of the group praised for smartness dropped compared with their scores on the first test, whereas the scores of the group praised for effort increased.[24]

So what is the take-away from all this research? Although it is well-intentioned, when offering praise, do your best to avoid praising your child using the following language: "You are the best! You are awesome! You are so smart!" This could backfire and result in your child's believing that if he doesn't do well on a task in the future, he's not smart. In contrast, it's better to praise a child for the process in which he's engaged, such as his effort or attention to the task. This will increase the chances that your toddler will grow up to embrace a *growth mindset*. Always praise for hard work and effort, not for intelligence. When your toddler struggles with a task and doesn't give up, praise him for sticking with it and working hard. Let you child know that intelligence is not fixed and that we all have the potential to grow and improve! By doing this, you are setting your toddler up for future happiness, fulfillment, and success.

One, Two, Buckle My Shoe

One, two,

Buckle my shoe.

Three, four,

Shut the door.

Five, six,

Pick up sticks.

Seven, eight,

Don't be late.

Nine, ten,

Do it over again!

Grit

Is there anything that parents can do to increase the chances that their child will reach his full potential? To answer this question, we need to delve into the research by Angela Duckworth. Dr Duckworth is a psychologist and scientist who has been involved in a number of research studies that relate to working hard and fulfilling potential. Her primary research interest is *grit*. *Grit* is defined as the ability to persevere and work to achieve one's goals over a long period.[25] Dr Duckworth's research is extensive. She has studied elementary school children, national spelling bee champions, West Point cadets, and successful sales-people. Can you guess what they all have in common? You've got it. *Grit!*

The students in her studies who excelled in school over-came struggles and put forth consistent effort, and the children who advanced to the finals in the spelling bee studied longer and harder than did their opponents. The West Point cadets who stayed in the program and did not drop out were hard-working and driven, and the salespeople who were successful were persistent and committed. Success was not about who had the most talent or the highest IQ. It was about who had the most *grit.*

Children who are willing to put forth consistent effort to meet their goals over an extended period have *grit.* They persist even after failing, and they are hard workers. Obviously, *grit* is a trait that we want our children to acquire. For some children, *grit* comes naturally, but for others, this is not the case.[25]

Developing Grit

It is important to challenge your child and teach him to persevere when the going gets tough. Every task should not be a "walk in the park." Allow your toddler to learn from his mistakes and to face and overcome obstacles. That means you shouldn't rush in and rescue him! Struggles are OK, and so are failures. All children need to learn how to deal with setbacks and failing, because both of these are part of real life. Keep in mind that failing is part of the learning process. Believe it or not, your child will learn how to pick himself up, dust himself off, and continue to strive toward his goal, and your role is to always be there for him and encourage him.

To help our children develop *grit,* it is also important to encourage them to take on difficult tasks. Parents should explain how challenges and struggles are learning opportunities, and that putting forth effort over the long run pays off. For example, if a puzzle looks extra-challenging and your child shies away from it, encourage him to give it a shot. Of course, modeling is another way to foster *grit* in children. As a parent, if you always strive toward your long-term goals in the face of adversity, your child will see this and learn from your example. Eventually, when your child faces a daunting task, you may hear him exclaim, "I love a challenge!"

Self-control

You may be wondering if there is a difference between *grit* and *self-control.* As you just read, *grit* is the ability to persevere to reach long-term goals, whereas *self-control* refers to the skill of regulating one's emotions, behaviors, and impulses in an immediate situation. Interestingly, even though *self-control* and *grit* seem to be very similar, not all individuals who have *self-control* are gritty, and vice versa. Yet Dr Duckworth believes that *grit* and *self-control* go hand in hand.

If you ask any parent, "What do you want for your child?", you will likely hear the following response: "I want my child to be happy." But how can a parent ensure happiness for a child? Obviously, there are no guarantees or cut-and-dried answers, but delving into the research may produce some ideas. For example, a landmark study initiated in the 1970s indicated that *self-control* was an important factor in attaining happiness. In fact, researchers in this long-term study discovered that high levels of *self-control* at a young age predicted greater health and success in adulthood. This makes perfect sense, because when we think of someone with no *self-control,* we tend to think of individuals who eat too much, drink too much, spend too much, and overindulge in general. These are definitely not healthy life habits!

Those findings are consistent with the results of another classic research study, often referred to as the "marshmallow study." In this investigation, preschool children were presented with a treat, such as a marshmallow. Each child was given the option of eating the treat immediately or waiting while the researcher left the room for approximately 15 minutes, and when the investigator returned, the preschooler would be given 2 treats. If the child could not wait to eat the treat, he only needed to ring a bell to call the researcher back to the room early, but that meant that he would not get the second treat. The preschoolers were basically being asked to delay gratification by maintaining *self-control.* One group of children was told that they could distract themselves by thinking about something fun while the investigator was out; others were told they could play with an available toy; and a third group was not given the distraction options. The results revealed that the children who played with the toy or distracted themselves with fun thoughts were more likely to delay gratification and earn the 2 marshmallows than were those who did not use a distractor.[26]

Truth Be Told

Research suggests that young children delay gratification longer for a large reward than for a small reward.[27]

A-Tisket, A-Tasket

A-tisket, a-tasket,

A green and yellow basket.

I wrote a letter to my love,

And on the way I dropped it,

I dropped it, I dropped it,

And on the way I dropped it.

A little boy, he picked it up,

And put it in his pocket.

During a follow-up study conducted when the children were adolescents, the investigators took a variety of measures. The researchers discovered that the preschoolers who were able to delay gratification longer had grown into adolescents who demonstrated superior academic performance, exhibited more *self-control,* and handled stress better than the children who had been unable to wait and had settled for just one treat.[26] Interestingly, the participants who had held out for 2 treats continued to demonstrate superior *self-control* as adults.[28]

Strategies and Activities for Teaching Self-control

Breathe In, Breathe Out: When your toddler is getting frustrated about something, show him how to take a slow deep breath in while you count "1-2-3 in," and a slow breath out, "1-2-3 out."

Still as a Statue! Challenge your child to "freeze" in a specific position. For example, show him how to hold both thumbs up, then encourage him to hold perfectly still while you count to 5. Gradually work your way up to a count of 20.

The Distraction Game: If your child is having difficulty waiting, encourage him to sing a favorite song, hum a tune, or look at an interesting item. Distracting oneself can be an effective strategy when there is a need to delay gratification.

Talk It Through: If your toddler is struggling with a task, teach him to use his words to figure it out. Tell him, "That looks like a tough problem. How can you solve that problem? What could you do next that might be helpful?"

The Freeze Frame Game: Turn on some lively music and dance with your child. When you stop the music, you both must freeze. See who can hold still the longest without wiggling or giggling. Try it again!

Tap to a Beat: If you and your toddler are stuck in a doctor's office waiting room, try playing "Tap to a Beat." Tap out a rhythm using your feet and see if your child can copy the rhythm. Gradually make the pattern more complex so that he will continue to be challenged.

Self-control Cue Cards: Cut out 3 construction paper circles, 1 red, 1 green, and 1 yellow. Laminate the circles to make them sturdy. Carry the cards with you and use them as visual prompts to help your child wait. For example, have him hold the red card in his hand while he waits in a line. When it is close to his turn, give him the yellow card so that he'll know he's getting close. Pass him the green circle when it's his turn!

So what is the best way for parents to increase the likelihood that their child will attain happiness? These findings suggest that young children need to be able to delay gratification and demonstrate *self-control* for future happiness. But can *self-control* be taught? The answer is yes! Use the strategies and activities provided in this chapter to promote the development of *self-control* in your toddler.

As a parent, you now know that *self-control* is important for your child's future happiness and academic success. You also know that intelligence and creativity can be developed in your child when you praise for effort rather than smartness. By striving toward your goals in a consistent manner and not giving up in the face of adversity, you are modeling *grit* for your toddler; this will, in turn, help him develop *grit* himself. And instilling a passion for hard work and determination in your child means the sky will be the limit!

CHAPTER 4

Why Old-fashioned Play Is Critical During the Toddler Years

CHAPTER 4

Why Old-fashioned Play Is Critical During the Toddler Years

Play is the work of children.

~ Jean Piaget

Children learn about the world and develop life skills through play. When a child plays, it benefits her social skills, her *dexterity,* and her cognitive, physical, and emotional health. And the icing on the cake is that play is fun! Unfortunately, many children these days are overscheduled and have limited opportunities for free, unstructured play. Also, concerns about safety may prevent children from having the freedom to explore the outdoors. These concerns can be addressed by taking appropriate precautions, such as slathering on the sunscreen before heading outdoors and watching out for safety hazards during outside play. As parents, we must provide ample time and opportunities for our children to play. This chapter highlights the benefits of play in early childhood and explains how parents can support and encourage playfulness.

A 2011 study documented a reduction in disruptive behavior in children after time spent playing.[29]

Types of Play

Play evolves during childhood. When a young toddler explores and plays independently, this is called *solitary play*. During this first stage of play, the child is often so engrossed in what she is doing that she doesn't notice what is going on around her. At about 2 years of age, toddlers begin to play alongside other children, but not with them. This second stage of play is called *parallel play*. During *parallel play*, a child may be aware of other children playing nearby, but no interaction occurs. Finally, *social play* (also called "cooperative play") begins to emerge around age 3 or 3½ years. This third stage of play involves children collaborating and working toward a common goal. *Social play* is interactive, and it often involves taking turns, solving problems, and acting out pretend scenarios.

Forms of Play

Children engage in different forms of play. Three forms of play are *physical, constructive, and pretend play,* and all of them are important for child development. *Physical play* offers opportunities for movement and exercise, and, in turn, the physical activity promotes health and wellness. *Constructive play* is more organized and goal-directed and involves building and creating. When a child builds a structure out of blocks, she is engaging in *constructive play.* Once a child gains experience with *physical play* and *constructive play, pretend or symbolic play* is next to emerge. This form of play includes role-playing and dramatization, so you may observe your child pretending to feed her doll and acting out a "Mommy" role. Think about it. When a child pretends, she engages her imagination and uses symbolism. No doubt, *pretend play* is a wonderful way to practice planning, organizing, remembering, and problem-solving! Let's look a little more closely at each form.

Physical Play

Physical play often takes place outdoors, and when a child is outside, she can move about freely and connect with nature. The great outdoors is full of interesting textures, rich smells, and fascinating sounds, which provide your toddler with a much-needed multisensory experience. Watch as she crumbles dry leaves, smells a sprig of honeysuckle, listens to a woodpecker pecking a tree, or experiences the warmth of the sun on her skin. She can run at full speed in open spaces, play on the playground, ride her bicycle, and breathe in the fresh air. This is how your child will learn to love being active. No doubt, it is critical that toddlers participate in physically active play to promote healthy development.

> **Truth Be Told**
>
> Outdoor playtime is associated with a reduced risk of nearsightedness.[30]

As a parent, do your best to expose your toddler to natural environments whenever possible. Why? Research suggests that exposure to nature is associated with improved cognitive skills, such as increased attentiveness and improved working memory. Also, when families live near a park, mothers report their children as healthier than do mothers who do not live near a green space.[31] If your family doesn't have easy access to a park, it is worth the effort to visit one when time allows, because when children spend time outdoors, they have better cardiovascular health, are more physically active, and have healthier weights.[32] Playing actively outdoors also raises vitamin D levels, which benefits a child's heart and bone health. So the next time you have a free afternoon, consider taking your toddler to the park.

> **Truth Be Told**
>
> Children who spend time in green spaces have fewer conduct problems, better peer relationships, and improved sleep.[33]

Believe it or not, there are even more reasons that young children should spend time in nature. Exploring the outdoors is a natural stress reducer, and exposure to green spaces has even been found to reduce the symptoms of attention-deficit/hyperactivity disorder in children. In one study, researchers discovered that memory and attention to task improved by 20% after the participants spent time in a natural outdoor setting.[34] Additional benefits of being physically active outdoors include improved motor skills, coordination, balance, and flexibility. It's important for parents to be aware that natural settings provide opportunities for creative play as well as quiet time, which are both important for young children. So take a nature walk with your child when the weather is nice and give her space to explore the natural surroundings. As you see, engaging in active movement outdoors on a regular basis is essential for your toddler's health and well-being.

You Are My Sunshine

You are my sunshine,
My only sunshine.
You make me happy
when skies are gray.
You'll never know, dear,
How much I love you,
Please don't take my sunshine away.

Constructive Play

It's no big surprise that toddlers love boxes. Just watch any child at a birthday party! Once she's unwrapped her toys, she'll likely start playing with the boxes the toys came in. When a child manipulates materials to build something new, she is participating in *constructive play.* Not only do toddlers have fun during *constructive play,* but the act of building has many developmental benefits. For example, block construction is a wonderful way to learn directional concepts such as "beside," "on top of," "over," and "under." When a child builds with various materials, it exercises her *fine motor skills* and her manipulative skills. An added bonus is that *constructive play* offers opportunities for your toddler to learn how to entertain herself, and the ability to entertain oneself is a critical life skill. Young children who occupy their time

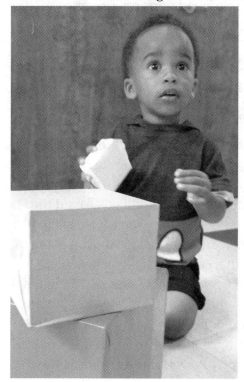

by engaging in self-directed, independent play are less likely to complain of boredom. So save your empty containers from the pantry, such as cereal boxes and oatmeal canisters, and watch your toddler have a blast while stacking and building! Be sure to look for any sharp or thin edges to guard against cuts.

Constructive play is also beneficial for *visual perceptual skills.* These skills are how the brain makes sense of the information the eyes take in and gives that information meaning (for example, recognizing a shape or finding a toy in a toybox). Visual perceptual processing is different from *visual acuity,* which is how clearly the eyes focus and see. Strong *visual perceptual skills* are important for writing, reading, drawing, working math problems, and many other day-to-day skills. Be sure to provide your child with empty boxes, blocks, and other items that are appropriate for *constructive play.*

Truth Be Told

Playing with puzzles on a regular basis in early childhood is associated with improved performance on visual-spatial tasks.[35]

Pretend Play

Around 18 to 24 months of age, young children begin to pretend during play, and with time they begin to plan imaginary scenarios ahead of time and act them out later. It is so exciting to see a young child engage in *pretend play!* On a lovely fall afternoon, I was visiting with a neighbor while her 2-year-old daughter, Elise, toddled around the backyard. I noticed Elise looking at a water hose lying on the ground. I approached Elise and said, "Are you going to water the flowers?" With a confused look on her face, Elise glanced around the yard. "No flowers," she said. "Oh, no!" I replied. "You are right—there aren't any flowers out here. Let's pretend!" I picked up the hose and pointed it at the empty flowerbed while making a spraying sound. "Look at me. I'm watering the pretty flowers. Spray, spray, spray."

Elise giggled and said, "My turn!" I passed the hose to her, and she began to imitate my actions. Then she smiled broadly and said, "Look, Mommy, I pretend!"

Truth Be Told

One research study found an association between mother-child *pretend play* during toddlerhood and higher IQs at age 5 years.[36]

During *pretend play,* toddlers actively use their imaginations and take on different roles. For example, your daughter may use a Frisbee as a steering wheel while pretending to be a truck driver. When a toddler is pretending, she is actually thinking symbolically. For example, she may imagine that a stick is a magic wand, a small box is a telephone, or a chair is her boat and the floor a lake. When I was a child, my best friend and I loved to pretend to be kittens attending school. We called it "kittygarten." When a child uses her imagination, the sky is the limit!

Play and Creativity

Play is important for instilling creativity in young children. When a toddler engages in creative play, she can be any character or any inanimate object she desires to be! During unstructured play, a child enters a state of mind that is conducive to creative thinking, and creative play often leads to innovation, critical thinking, and problem-solving. As adults, we know that a big part of life is dealing with problems and coming up with solutions to those problems. Think about it. To come up with solutions, we tap into our creativity on a daily basis. This is also true for your toddler. Without a doubt, children need regular opportunities to think creatively.

Creative Activity: Make a Collage

Start with a blank piece of paper or poster board. Have your child use fabric, images from magazines, and yarn or string to create a fun collage. Encourage her to use her imagination!

Can I Promote Creativity in My Child?

Yes! Research suggests that collaboration, dialogue, and unstructured play are important for creativity. In one research study, a group of children who were given an opportunity to freely play with salt dough before completing a craft activity demonstrated more creativity than did another group of children who copied text from a chalkboard before completing the same craft.[37] In another study, children created artwork depicting a variety of emotions, and after creating the art, they were given the opportunity to talk about their work. The children who participated in the study increased their creativity and emotional awareness.[38] It seems that producing art related to emotions helps a child get in touch with her feelings. Take note of the following suggestions for promoting creativity in your toddler.

Promote Creativity

- Provide opportunities for your child to engage her natural curiosity and occupy her time with enjoyable activities on a daily basis.

- Allow for mistakes!

- Encourage your toddler to channel her emotions into her artwork.

- Ask open-ended questions.

- Have a wide array of supplies available when crafting, and allow your child to choose the materials that she prefers and that will engage her senses.

- Encourage your child to create artwork that depicts emotions such as happiness, sadness, anger, and fear and ask her to describe her creation.

- Don't feel the need to constantly entertain your toddler. Remember, boredom stimulates creativity!

Digging It!

If you are planting flowers in your yard, allow your toddler to join in the fun. Give her a sturdy plastic spoon and two containers, and show her how to scoop the dirt and transfer it from one container to the next. Who knows—she might even want to make a mud pie!

Play and Social Skills

All of the types and forms of play we've reviewed in this chapter have social benefits. When playing with peers, your toddler has to follow social rules, be adaptable, communicate her desires, and make her needs known. For example, if she wants to join a friend who is playing with a set of interlocking blocks, that would be the perfect opportunity to use her language skills and ask to join in. When playing with peers, your child will begin to understand how others feel, and showing compassion and empathy is foundational for forming friendships. When interacting with friends, a toddler also begins to learn how to regulate her emotions. If a peer snatches your child's toy, her first instinct may be to scream, lash out in anger, or take the toy back. If she reacts in that manner, it is appropriate to step in and model an appropriate reaction such as, "I can see that you are very upset because Billy took your doll. Why don't you tell Billy that you were playing with the doll, and you would like it back? Maybe you could even let Billy hold your baby doll once you finish feeding her." By teaching your toddler how to use her words in such situations, she will begin to learn how to resolve conflict in an appropriate manner. When playing with peers, your child has opportunities to communicate, cooperate with others, and socialize appropriately.

The Itsy-Bitsy Spider

The itsy-bitsy spider
Climbed up the waterspout.
Down came the rain
And washed the spider out.
Out came the sun
And dried up all the rain,
And the itsy-bitsy spider
Climbed up the spout again.

Truth Be Told

Before the age of 2 years, group play may be challenging for a child because she is not developmentally ready to share her toys.[39] In her mind, everything is hers!

Family Play

Do you remember as a kid when you laughed so hard your sides would hurt? Many adults have forgotten how much joy can be experienced while playing. Keep in mind that you can join your child in play at any time! It's easy. Just follow her lead as her natural curiosity prompts her to explore her surroundings. During your time together, be present and engaged, and make a point to be silly with your little one. By tapping into your "inner child," you will both have fun, you'll relieve some stress, and the bond between the two of you will grow.

Toddlers are on a mission to make sense of the world, and they do this through active play and exploration. As a parent, how can you ensure that your child has ample opportunities to play? First, limit screen time and encourage outdoor play. Your toddler will benefit so much more from making a mud pie out in the fresh air than playing a video game. Also, provide items and materials that foster play, such as paper, crayons, dress-up clothing, salt dough, and finger paints. By playing actively, your child will gain strength, develop her mind, and experience a multitude of additional growth opportunities.

Research reveals that free play in childhood fosters language, math, reading, and social skills.[40]

CHAPTER 5

How Screen Time and Digital Media Use Are Affecting Today's Young Children

CHAPTER 5

How Screen Time and Digital Media Use Are Affecting Today's Young Children

The human spirit must prevail over technology.

~ Albert Einstein

Parenting a toddler has been compared to riding a roller coaster. It has its ups and downs, and the responsibility can be challenging, exciting, and exhausting all at the same time. As parents, we want to make the best decisions so that we set our children up for success—but how are we supposed to know the right decisions to make when it comes to technology exposure during the toddler years? The stakes are high. Research suggests that the overuse of technology may lead to sleep problems and behavior issues, and children who are overexposed to media are also at risk of becoming obese. Yet, as we know, young children are spending more and more time with devices these days, and because technology is here to stay, many parents want their children to gain technology skills early in life. But rest assured—there's plenty of time for kids to become tech savvy.

As we know, toddlers are dependent on their caregivers when it comes to screen time exposure, so parents must guide their children when it comes to media use. Parents these days have extremely busy schedules and are often exhausted and overcome with responsibilities. There may be evenings when allowing a child to engage in screen time provides parents with the downtime that they so desperately need. This chapter provides research-based information for parents to consider when setting screen-time and digital media–use guidelines for their toddlers.

Shockingly, more than 30% of babies play with a mobile device for the first time while in diapers.[41]

The Allure of the Television

You have a load of laundry to fold, the dishwasher needs emptying, and it's almost dinnertime. You haven't started cooking, and your toddler is following you from room to room asking for a snack. The first solution that pops into your mind is to turn on the television and tempt your little one with a child-friendly show. And this won't be difficult, with all the programming created just for babies these days! However, do your best to resist this temptation, especially if your child is younger than 2 years. Why? There are a number of reasons, and we will cover them in this chapter. The American Academy of Pediatrics recommends not exposing infants and toddlers younger than 18 months to TV and other entertainment media, other than video chatting. See the American Academy of Pediatrics Recommendations for Children's Media Use box later in this chapter.

Truth Be Told

Research reveals that free play in childhood fosters language, math, reading, and social skills.[40]

When I was a child, there were very few TV programs created just for children. In fact, I always looked forward to Saturday mornings, because that was the only day cartoons were on! But the children's programming landscape began to shift, and by 1990, the creation of television programs for children had increased so greatly that Congress passed the Children's Television Act. Through this act, legislators set out to improve the quality of informational and educational shows for children. The act also placed restrictions on advertising during children's programming. Oh, how times have changed! Now, in the digital media age, there are 24-hour channels dedicated to programming for young children, toddlers, and even babies.

Believe it or not, these days children between the ages of 12 and 24 months spend more than 2 hours a day in front of screens, and approximately 35% of toddlers have a TV in their bedroom.[42] However, it's not just toddlers who are exposed to screen time. Approximately 40% of parents report that their 3-month-olds watch TV or videos on a regular basis.[43]

Truth Be Told

Early viewing of violent television programming is associated with antisocial behavior, inattention, and lower academic achievement.[44]

Unfortunately, many parents are misinformed when it comes to their beliefs about young children's screen exposure. For example, in one study, 78% of parents felt that TV viewing was an appropriate distraction for children, and 59% were not concerned about the amount of their children's screen time. In fact, most parents believe that TVs, computers, and tablets have a positive influence on children's education and creativity, despite the fact that there is no solid research to substantiate these beliefs.[45] The truth is that screen time can have a negative influence on cognitive and language development, and excessive screen time is associated with attention and memory limitations, as well as with poor math and reading achievement.[46,47]

American Academy of Pediatrics Recommendations for Children's Media Use

"For children younger than 18 months, avoid use of screen media other than video-chatting. Parents of children 18 to 24 months of age who want to introduce digital media should choose high-quality programming, and watch it with their children to help them understand what they're seeing."[48]

Once your toddler reaches the age of 18 to 24 months, it is possible for him to learn from quality programming developed just for children, as long as a parent is involved with him while he is viewing the content. When you watch a well-designed child-friendly show with your little one, it is important to explain what the child is seeing, label items, and ask open-ended questions about the various scenarios on the screen.[49] This allows your child to make meaning out of what he sees, which is how learning occurs.

> **Truth Be Told**
>
> In a study of children seen in an urban, low-income, minority community pediatric clinic, 97% of the children's households had televisions, 77% had smartphones, and 83% had tablets.[50]

Background Noise

Do you typically have the TV on while cooking dinner or cleaning the house? Many parents have a habit of doing this, even if they aren't watching a particular show. What we may not realize is that our little ones are often paying attention to the screen even if we are not. On average, babies ranging in age from 8 to 24 months are exposed to more than 5 hours of background TV every day.[51] Yet, research suggests that having a TV on in the room limits how often and how well parents interact with their toddlers.[52] Parents have fewer conversations with their children when the TV is on, speaking 500 to 1,000 words fewer each hour than when the TV is off.[53] This is of concern because language exposure is extremely beneficial for infant development—and every word you speak to your child is important! Why? Studies have shown that the more in-person communication to which infants are exposed early in life, the better their vocabularies will be and the greater their chances of future academic success.[54]

This Old Man

This old man, he played one,
He played knick-knack on my thumb.
Knick-knack paddywhack,
give your dog a bone,
This old man came rolling home.

This old man, he played two,
He played knick-knack on my shoe.
Knick-knack paddywhack,
give your dog a bone,
This old man came rolling home.

This old man, he played three,
He played knick-knack on my knee.
Knick-knack paddywhack,
give your dog a bone,
This old man came rolling home.

This old man, he played four,
He played knick-knack on my door.
Knick-knack paddywhack,
give your dog a bone,
This old man came rolling home.

This old man, he played five,
He played knick-knack on my hive.
Knick-knack paddywhack,
give your dog a bone,
This old man came rolling home.

This Old Man (continued)

This old man, he played six,
He played knick-knack on my sticks.
Knick-knack paddywhack,
give your dog a bone,
This old man came rolling home.

This old man, he played seven,
He played knick-knack up in heaven.
Knick-knack paddywhack,
give your dog a bone,
This old man came rolling home.

This old man, he played eight,
He played knick-knack on my gate.
Knick-knack paddywhack,
give your dog a bone,
This old man came rolling home.

This old man, he played nine,
He played knick-knack on my spine.
Knick-knack paddywhack,
give your dog a bone,
This old man came rolling home.

This old man, he played ten,
He played knick-knack once again.
Knick-knack paddywhack,
give your dog a bone,
This old man came rolling home.

The negative effects of background TV are not limited to parent-child interaction and communication. If a 12- to 36-month old child is playing in a room with a TV on in the background, research reveals that he has limited focus and plays less, even if the toy is new.[55] Also, children younger than 24 months often watch violent or inappropriate background content that is intended for adults.[56] The bottom line is that background TV is not useful in your child's development. It is definitely worth turning the TV off, especially if you aren't watching it. Additionally, experts recommend that every home should have screen-free zones. These are areas and times in which no screens are allowed, such as during family meals and in the bedroom.

The Allure of Tablets and Smartphones

The next time you are eating in a restaurant, take a look around. You will likely observe multiple children at nearby tables who are absorbed by screens! And think about how often you pass a car and notice that the children in the backseat are all engaged with technology.

> **Truth Be Told**
>
> In 2011, only 8% of young US families owned a tablet computer. By 2013, the percentage had risen to 40%.[42]

Marketers would have you believe that the time a young child spends on a tablet or smartphone is beneficial for learning. Believe it or not, approximately 80,000 apps are marketed as "educational." However, there is limited research to confirm these claims.[57] Still, babies as young as 12 months often have access to their parents' devices, and by 2 years of age, most tots are skilled with touch screens and interact purposefully with these devices.[58] Yet, when young children swipe and click on a device, it doesn't necessarily mean they are learning. In fact, when babies spend time on tablets and touch screens, they communicate less with others and, thus, are hindered in their language development. They also miss out on opportunities to entertain themselves, and when a child entertains himself, he is learning self-regulation skills. See Chapter 4.

Well-designed touch screen apps may allow for learning opportunities for young children. If the content is developmentally appropriate and interactive and a parent is involved in the child's interaction with the content, studies have found that gains in vocabulary development are possible.[59] The key is for parents to be informed and to carefully consider the content they allow their children to view. Resources such as PBS Kids, Sesame Workshop, and Common Sense Media provide resources for parents who are looking for quality products.[60]

Smart Toys

One would think that electronic toys are just what a toddler needs. The lights, sounds, and buttons seem to be stimulating and fun. Yet, when a parent and child interact with an electronic book together, the parent reads less and speaks fewer words to the child as compared with when they use print books.[61] Why? It seems that parents rely on the toy to speak and, therefore, they say less. Traditional toys and books offer more opportunities for parents to describe, explain, point to pictures, and have a dialogue with their little ones, which is exactly what your child needs! That means there's no pressure to buy expensive electronic toys for your toddler. Just stick with the tried and true traditional toys, such as building blocks and puzzles. These good old-fashioned toys promote creativity and are great for your child's visual motor skills.

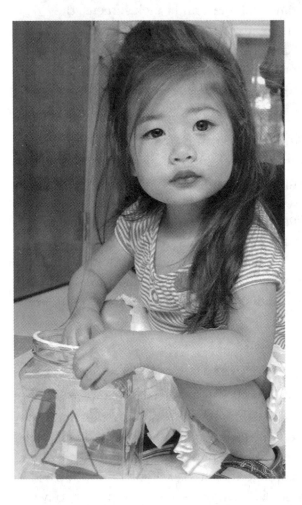

Screen Time's Effects on Sleeping and Eating

"Mommy, I'm sleepy." If you hear this phrase frequently, your child may not be getting enough quality sleep. Be aware that excessive screen time has a negative impact on a child's sleep, and having a TV in the bedroom increases the risk of sleep problems. Also, violent programming watched during the day negatively influences sleep quality.[62] To ensure that your little one gets the quality sleep that is critical for development, avoid screen time in the evening, especially in the hour before bedtime, and keep the TV out of his bedroom.

In addition to causing sleep issues, too much screen time can lead to weight gain in children. Why? The time spent in front of the TV replaces time that could be spent being physically active. Also, when tuned in to the screen, children are exposed to marketing for junk food, and they often eat unhealthy snacks and beverages while watching TV, even if they are not hungry.[63] In recent years, obesity has reached epidemic proportions across the globe, so it is important for parents to expose children to a home environment that supports obesity prevention by limiting screen time.

Brother John

Are you sleeping,
Are you sleeping,
Brother John,
Brother John?
Morning bells are ringing,
Morning bells are ringing.
Ding, dang, dong!
Ding, dang, dong!

Truth Be Told

Children who live in poverty are especially vulnerable to the negative effects of media.[64]

Video Chatting

Not all technology poses risks to toddlers. Yes! This is good news! Videophone apps provide wonderful opportunities for real-life encounters with grandparents or other family members whom your child doesn't get to see often. This interaction allows your child to visit with loved ones, practice social interaction, and gain language skills.[65] The key is that parents need to be involved and actively participating during the video chats so that their toddlers can understand what they are seeing and hearing.[60]

Moving Forward

As we know, toddlers are constantly watching parents and modeling our actions, and it's important to keep this in mind when it comes to media exposure and screen time. For example, research tells us that that the more a mother watches television, the more time her child will spend viewing TV,[66] so it's important to model reasonable television viewing. Screen time is also habit-forming, so if your child starts engaging with media early, it will be more difficult for him to break bad screen habits as he gets older. And the more frequently your child relies on screen time for entertainment, the more dependent he will become on screens.[67]

> **Truth Be Told**
>
> The American Academy of Pediatrics recommends that all families develop a family media use plan. Visit www.healthychildren.org/MediaUsePlan for specific guidelines.

Through reading this chapter, you've learned that media exposure for children aged 24 months and younger should be avoided. Rarely, technology can be a learning tool for children older than 18 months, especially if a parent interacts with the child during screen time.[60] You've also learned that it is extremely important for parents take content into consideration when setting media guidelines for their children.[46] There are several resources that parents may find helpful when making these important decisions. TV Parental Guidelines (www.tvguidelines.org) rate programs on the basis of the themes and age-appropriateness of the content. The Entertainment Software Rating Board (www.esrb.org) also assigns age and content ratings to video games and apps.

Toddlers and young children learn best during hands-on play and during rich, positive social interaction with family

and caregivers. Not only are these interactions fun and beneficial for child development, but also they provide wonderful opportunities for parents and children to bond and connect.

CHAPTER 6

Enhancing Development With Retro Activities: 12 to 18 Months

CHAPTER 6

Enhancing Development With Retro Activities: 12 to 18 Months

Your children will become what you are,
so be what you want them to be.

~ David Bly

Once your baby starts to walk, she is officially a toddler! Now that your little one is mobile, her horizons are expanding, and she's beginning to develop a sense of autonomy. As she starts to think for herself, she will likely want to venture out and explore the environment as much as possible, and it is through this exploration that she continues to learn about the world around her. Toddlers are innately curious, so keep a close eye on her just in case she gets into any mischief! By keeping her safe while allowing her to venture out and discover the world, you are supporting her learning and development.

Play Time and Toys

A wonderful way to bond with your toddler is through play, but don't feel pressure to spend a lot of money at the toy store. Browsing in the toy section can be intimidating, to say the least. Many toy manufacturers report that their products stimulate development, but this is not always accurate. When selecting toys for your toddler, steer clear of the fancy electronic options and keep an eye out for old-school toys that are interesting and colorful. Simple toys can be useful for teaching vocabulary and a variety of concepts and, to top it off, they are fun!

This chapter provides a variety of stimulating play activities that are developmentally appropriate for a 12- to 18-month-old. As you carry out these activities with your toddler, take advantage of teachable moments. You will be supporting her desire to learn while strengthening the connection between the two of you.

Developmental Milestones: 12 to 18 Months

- Stacks 3 or 4 blocks or other items to make a tower
- Points to at least one body part
- Places items into a container and removes them
- Engages in *parallel play* (side-by-side with limited interaction)
- Walks holding furniture or independently
- Drinks from a cup
- Says "mama," "dada," and "uh-oh"
- Says several single words
- Attempts to imitate words

- Is fearful or anxious around strangers
- Assists with dressing by extending arms and legs
- Imitates simple actions or gestures
- May engage in simple *pretend play*
- Scribbles on paper without demonstration
- Finds hidden items[68,69]

Toy Tips: 12 to 18 Months

- Blocks for stacking and building
- Board books
- Sorting and *nesting* toys
- Small plastic shovel and bucket
- Soft balls of large sizes
- Push and pull toys with wheels
- Toy shopping cart
- Shape sorter
- Large wooden beads for stringing
- Basic knob puzzles
- Age-appropriate construction toys

Dealing With Separation Anxiety

Around 18 months of age, your toddler may start to have a difficult time separating from you. It can be stressful and heart-wrenching to leave your little one during a tearful goodbye. The following may make the separation process more bearable.

- Always tell your toddler when you are leaving. Avoid sneaking out.

- Don't drag out saying goodbye. Consistently stick with a brief "bye-bye" and a quick kiss. This will decrease the length of the separation, and the routine will make parting easier for your toddler.

- Don't engage in a dialogue with your child during the transition. Simply state when you will return before saying goodbye.

- Encourage your child to hold onto a comforting item, such as a favorite blanket, during the departure. This may help ease her anxiety.

- Be aware that separation anxiety often intensifies if a child is ill, sleepy, or hungry. Significant life changes such as a new baby, a house move, or a vacation can also make separation challenging.

Developing Skill: Pincer Grasp

Parents are typically excited when their toddler's *gross motor skills* begin to advance. Walking, running, and jumping are definitely a big deal, but *fine motor skills* are important too! You may have noticed that your toddler is starting to use the tips of her thumb and index finger to grasp small items. This is called a *pincer grasp.* Previously, she probably used her fingers to rake tiny items into her palm to pick them up, but now that she is developing finger isolation, she will start using a *pincer grasp.* This makes finger feeding and using other *fine motor skills* much easier for your child! Think of how much independence your little one will gain once she can open small containers, hold a spoon correctly, and zip a zipper. As your toddler grasps and manipulates small items in the environment, she is naturally developing her *fine motor skills.*

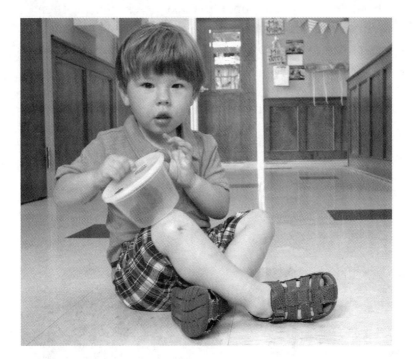

Activities to Improve a Pincer Grasp

The following activities are great for developing your toddler's *pincer grasp.*

Activity 1: Fancy Fingers

When snack time comes around, keep an ice tray handy. Place individual pieces of finger food in each section of the ice tray. Your toddler will have to use her thumb and index finger to retrieve each piece. This might be slightly challenging at first, so feel free to give her some direction or assistance if needed.

Activity 2: Lace the Day Away

Make your toddler her very own lacing cards by using colorful poster board and a shoelace. Cut the lacing card into the shape of your choice, such as a heart, a square, or a triangle. Use a hole punch to make holes, spacing them evenly around the border of the shape. Give your child the lace and show her how to lace around the shape, threading the shoelace in and out of the holes. Make the lacing cards sturdier and easy to clean by laminating them. This is a wonderful activity for enhancing eye-hand coordination.

Activity 3: Drops of Color

Prepare colored water by mixing one-eighth cup of water with several drops of food coloring. Use 3 different colors, each in its own bowl. Have your child squeeze an eyedropper and fill it with one color at a time, then squeeze out several small drops of the colored water onto a coffee filter to make a lovely design. Be sure to tell her how proud you are of her creation! For more information on praise, see Chapter 3.

Activity 4: Noodle Fun

Have your toddler thread large uncooked pieces of manicotti pasta onto a piece of colorful ribbon. Not only does this give your child practice with her *pincer grasp* and eye-hand coordination, it requires sustained focus and attention to task. The completed product can be a bracelet or a necklace that she can wear or give as a gift.

The More We Get Together

Oh, the more we get together,
Together, together,
Oh, the more we get together,
The happier we'll be.
For your friends are my friends,
And my friends are your friends.
Oh, the more we get together,
The happier we'll be!

Developing Skill: Bilateral Use of Hands

You may have noticed that your toddler is starting to use both hands together in a somewhat coordinated manner. When this happens, she is demonstrating *bilateral skills.* Using the right and left sides of the body together occurs when crawling, walking, and writing. *Bilateral skills* develop in stages. The first stage is *symmetrical bilateral integration.* This is when both sides of a child's body carry out the same action at the same time, such as with clapping. *Reciprocal bilateral integration* skills follow when one side of the body moves in the opposite direction of the other side, as with crawling.

The next stage is *asymmetrical bilateral integration.* This stage is much more complicated, because each side of the body is carrying out a different pattern of movement. For example, unbuttoning and buttoning involve *asymmetrical bilateral integration.* Another stage of *bilateral skill* development is the ability to cross the *midline,* moving one arm or leg over to the opposite side of the body.[70] For example, when your toddler puts a toy bracelet on one wrist by using the opposite hand, she is crossing her *midline.* Check out the following activities that involve *bilateral skills.*

Activities to Promote Bilateral Skills

Activity 1: Open Sesame!

Collect a variety of small plastic jars for your child to practice opening and closing. When she first learns how to open a jar, the top should be slightly loose so that she can remove it easily. As she gains coordination and hand strength, your toddler will begin to remove and replace the lids with more ease. Motivate her to open the jar by placing a small treat inside for her to retrieve.

Activity 2: Scrunchies Are Fun

For this activity, you will need a toilet paper roll and several colorful ponytail holders or hair scrunchies. Show your toddler how to stretch open each scrunchie and place it around the toilet paper roll. She can alternate the colors to make a fun pattern. When she puts them all on, have her take them off and start over. This task is entertaining, and it's good for *bilateral skills.*

Activity 3: Be My Honey

For this activity, you will need a clean plastic honey bear container with the lid and a variety of colorful ribbons cut into 4- to 6-inch strips. Slowly place each ribbon through the small hole in the top of the honey bear container while your toddler watches. Now give her a turn. Watch as she concentrates and uses her eye-hand coordination to thread each ribbon through the hole. Be sure to praise her for working hard!

Activity 4: Rolling On

Do you have a rolling pin that you rarely use? If so, pull it out. Playing with a rolling pin is a wonderful way for your child to practice using both hands together in a coordinated way. Have her roll out a handful of Play-Doh into the shape of a pancake, then show her how to use a plastic cookie cutter to make a batch of pretend cookies. Or better yet, have her help bake real cookies!

Activity 5: Easy On, Easy Off

For this activity, you will need a cylindrical block or short dowel and several small terry cloth ponytail holders (available at most dollar stores). You and your child can take turns placing each ponytail holder on the dowel. Name the color of the ponytail holder as you put it on the dowel and encourage your toddler to do the same. She will learn her colors as she develops her eye-hand coordination. Always supervise your toddler when playing this game to ensure that she doesn't put the ponytail holders in her mouth.

When should I take the pacifier away?

Babies are born with the need to suck, which is important for eating and drinking. For babies, pacifiers help reduce the risk of sudden infant death syndrome (commonly referred to as SIDS). For a toddler, sucking on a pacifier is calming. When you decide to limit its use, do so gradually. This will give your little one opportunities to learn how to self-soothe in other ways, such as snuggling with a stuffed animal or holding a blanket tightly. By the time your child reaches 2 years, the pacifier should be a thing of the past. Sucking on a pacifier is associated with a heightened risk of ear infections, so if your toddler has a history of recurrent ear infections, you may want to get rid of the pacifier even earlier than 2 years. It is also important to know that prolonged use of a pacifier can lead to dental problems and issues with your toddler's bite. If you have concerns related to your child's teeth or bite, consult your pediatrician or a pediatric dentist.

Developing Skill: Object Permanence

Knowing that an object exists even when it is hidden from sight is called *object permanence*. Your child begins to develop this skill around 8 to 10 months of age and continues to develop it as she explores and experiences the world around her. This means that when you leave the room, although your toddler may cry, she knows that you still exist! The following activities require the skill of object permanence.

Activities to Promote Object Permanence Skills

Activity 1: You've Got Mail!

It is always a treat to check the mailbox and find a letter. Use a shoebox to make a pretend mailbox. Cut the edges of the top of the box about one-third of the distance from one end and fold the lid back. Tape the rest of the lid in place and cover the entire box with colorful adhesive paper. Place several pretend letters inside and encourage your child to open the lid and retrieve them. Ask her, "Do you have a note in the mailbox? Open it and see!" She will also enjoy "mailing" letters by opening the mailbox and placing each one inside. Imagine all the fun you and your toddler will have with this mailbox activity!

Activity 2: Backpack Bliss

Toddlers love backpacks with lots of pouches and zippers. A backpack is the perfect place for your child to store her favorite small toys and books. When she retrieves and replaces items, she will be practicing her zipper skills. The zipper pull should have a small hold at the tip. If your child has difficulty grasping the zipper with her thumb and finger, attach a key ring to the pull. This will make it less challenging for your child to grasp and pull the zipper. Have a special hook just for her backpack, and teach her to hang it up whenever she's not using it. She's already learning how to be neat and tidy!

Activity 3: Feely-Feely Game

When your toddler isn't looking, take a tube sock and place several small items inside the sock, such as a ping-pong ball, a plastic animal, and a small toy car. Ask her reach into the sock and use her sense of touch to locate the car. It may take her several attempts to identify and pull out the correct object, but she will have fun all the while.

Activity 4: Pocketbook Play

If you have an extra pocketbook or wallet around the house, don't get rid of it. Your toddler will have lots of fun playing with it! Make sure it has plenty of pockets and slots for photos and credit cards, and collect some of your old discount cards, photographs, and business cards for her to put in and remove. She will enjoy pulling the items out and putting them back in over and over again. She will also have fun telling you the names of the people in the photos.

Activity 5: Where Is the Toy?

Hide a small stuffed animal while your child isn't looking, leaving only a small portion of the toy visible. Turn off the lights and challenge your child to find the item by using a flashlight. When your child turns the flashlight on and off, say "on" and "off," and encourage her to imitate you. This will help her understand these concepts, and turning the flashlight on and off exercises *fine motor skills*. Once she finds the hidden item, hide it again and repeat the activity.

One, Two, Three, Four, Five

One, two, three, four, five,

Once I caught a fish alive.

Six, seven, eight, nine, ten,

Then I let it go again.

Why did you let it go?

Because it bit my finger so.

Which finger did it bite?

This little finger on my right.

Developing Skill: Joint Attention

When 2 individuals pay attention to an object, person, or experience, this is called "joint attention." You may not be familiar with the specific term, but you and your toddler engage in joint attention on a regular basis. For example, if your 18-month-old is interested in a nearby toy, she may look at the toy, then look at you to see if you are attending to the item. If you are not looking, your toddler might gaze back and forth between you and the toy, prompting you to attend to the toy. She may even point at it and glance at you in hopes of directing your gaze toward the toy. She is initiating joint attention! Keep in mind that both you and your toddler can initiate joint attention, and parents can encourage joint attention by gesturing and verbally prompting a child to look at any target object. Interestingly, joint attention provides a foundation for cognitive, language, and social skill development. Review the activities in the following section for ideas on improving joint attention skills.

Autism: Watch out for the Early Signs

It is important for parents to know the early signs of autism spectrum disorder. Early diagnosis is critical, because research tells us that intensive intervention in young children with autism has positive developmental effects.[71]

Here are some early signs that may be linked to autism:

- Demonstrates limited or no eye contact

- Does not use her finger to point at items

- Does not respond to her name when called

- Has limited ability to communicate

- Spins, rocks, wiggles fingers, or flaps her hands frequently

- Loses skills before 2 years of age that were previously present

- Has sensory sensitivities

- Does not respond to her name when called at 12 months[72]

If you have concerns about your toddler's development, consult your pediatrician.

Activities to Improve Joint Attention Skills

Activity 1: Do You See What I See?

Point to one of your child's favorite toys that is just out of reach and name it. Wait for her to turn her head to look at the toy. As soon as she locks her eyes on it, give her the toy. Repeat the process with another out-of-reach item and reward your child for following your lead again.

Activity 2: Brilliant Binoculars

Take two empty toilet paper rolls and cover each one with colorful duct tape. Use two extra strips of tape to secure the tubes together like a pair of binoculars. Challenge your child to find certain shapes or colors around the room using her binoculars. For example, ask her, "Can you find a square? Or, "Do you see anything in this room that is a square?" Give her a high five as soon as she locates each one correctly!

Activity 3: I Spy, You Spy

"I spy" is a trusted game that families often play while traveling in a car, but the fun does not have to be limited to a car ride. You can play this game at home in the traditional way, or add a twist by asking the child to locate an item that you describe but don't call by name. For example, have your child search for a tennis ball by saying, "I spy with my little eye something that is round and yellow." This is a wonderful way to introduce new descriptive words to your child's vocabulary.

Research reveals that when parents use verbal language along with gestures, it promotes longer periods of joint attention.[73]

Activity 4: Lookie-Lookie-Lookie

Sit on the floor with your child and offer her a toy. While she is playing with the toy, describe it and point to its different characteristics. You can also talk about what your child is doing—for example, "Look—you are rolling the toy car forward and backward." This is a wonderful way to increase your toddler's vocabulary and promote language development.

Activity 5: Your Turn, My Turn

Taking turns is an important skill that involves joint attention, and reading is a fun way to teach your toddler this skill. Using a sturdy board book, encourage your child to turn a page all by herself. Allow plenty of time for her to carry out her turn, then ask her, "Is it my turn now?" Once you have her attention, turn one page in an exaggerated manner. Say, "Look, now I am turning a page! Next, it will be your turn! Isn't it fun taking turns?" Your toddler will look at you and then look at the book. Remember, when the two of you share an interest in the book, this is called "joint attention."

> **Tips for Discipline**
>
> Spanking, shaking, and pinching a child are not appropriate ways to discipline a child. In fact, these actions can be harmful and may result in your toddler's becoming fearful or aggressive. The message that is sent with physical discipline is that it is OK to hurt another person. Instead, the American Academy of Pediatrics (AAP) recommends beginning with a loving, positive, and nurturing relationship with your child. The next recommendation is to use positive reinforcement to encourage desired behaviors from your child. The AAP also recommends the use of age-appropriate time-outs for your little one.[20] Be sure to speak with your pediatrician regarding any questions you have about discipline.

Developing Skill: Follows Simple Directions

Your toddler is gradually becoming more capable of following simple directions, and when she follows verbal directions, she is exercising her listening skills. The ability to follow basic directions is an important life skill. These activities will help your child improve her concentration and memory, which are important for following directions. An inability to follow simple directions may be a sign of a hearing problem, cognitive issues, or a receptive language disorder. If you have any of these concerns, consult your pediatrician.

Activities to Promote Verbal and Listening Skills

Activity 1: Fun With Sticky Notes
Place a yellow sticky note on a nearby item, then show your toddler another sticky note and ask her to look around the

room and find one just like it and bring it to you. Feel free to prompt her if she needs some help. For example, tell her, "It's near the green chair," or "It's close to the mirror." After she brings it to you, draw a smiley face on it and tell her, "Good job!"

Activity 2: Match Made in Heaven

You can make your toddler her very own matching game! Use a brightly colored permanent marker to draw a variety of shapes on the sides and bottom of a large clear plastic container. Cut from a thick craft foam sheet matching shapes that are the same size as the ones on the container. Add the loop side of Velcro sticky dots to the center of each foam shape and attach the hook side to the center of each shape on the inside of the plastic container. Ask your child to place each shape on the proper shape and watch her match away! Teach her about the concepts of "in" and "out" as she places and removes the shapes.

Truth Be Told

How you talk to your child is important for her vocabulary development. Using gestures and expressive glances will help her understand newly introduced concepts and words.[74]

Activity 3: Toy Box Labels

If your child's toys are all mixed together in a large toy box, it's time to get organized! How? Use separate storage bins for each category of toy. For example, all toy cars should go in one container, all building blocks in another, and all stuffed animals in a third. Take a photograph of a toy in each of the categories and laminate all the photos. Then attach each photo to a storage bin and you're all set!

Explain to your toddler that all the toys have special containers, and show her how to match the type of toy with the appropriate photo. The next time you tell her to put her toys away, she'll know exactly where they go.

Time-out Tips[75]

- Provide an explanation for time-out before using it, including the behaviors that will result in time-out, where it will take place, and when it will be used.

- Only use time-out when your toddler demonstrates dangerous behavior, hurts another person, or breaks a family rule. Use other discipline approaches for other undesired behaviors.

- The location of the time-out should not allow your child to gain attention from others or engage in play.

- Time-outs should range from 2 to 5 minutes, depending on the child's age.

Use the 5-step approach for all time-outs.

- Always give a warning when your child misbehaves—for example, "If you throw your toy on the floor again, you will go to time-out."

- Provide an explanation for the time-out: "You are going to time-out because you threw your toy on the floor."

- Your toddler should sit during the time-out, with no talking allowed.

- End the time-out after 1 minute for every year of your child's age.

- Praise your child the next time she behaves.

Activity 4: The Listening Game

Here is an activity that your toddler will truly enjoy! In my research, I've found that toddlers are fascinated with audio recordings, especially when the audio is of a familiar person. It promotes listening skills without the need to rely on visual skills. Use the audio recorder on your smart phone to record yourself giving your child instructions, then play the recording for her. For example, say, "Show me your nose," "Point to your ear," or "Stomp your foot." If she seems unsure of what to do, model the action for her. Once she catches on, she'll want you to record more and more messages. What a fun way to work on those listening skills!

Activity 5: Pop That Bubble!

It's time for bubble play! As your child visually follows a bubble with her eyes, use your index finger to point at it and follow the movement of the bubble with your hand. Encourage her to continue watching by saying, "Look!" You can also encourage her to point at the bubble with her index finger and then pop it.

Another Perspective

An interesting study that was carried out more than 10 years ago provides insight into how 14- to 18-month-old children are capable of taking the perspective of another person. Researchers gave the toddlers 2 bowls of food. One contained fresh broccoli and the other held goldfish crackers. The children tasted each food and either gestured or made expressions indicating whether they liked or disliked it. The investigators followed up by tasting each food and reacting with a disgusted or happy expression. Half of the time, the researchers matched their reactions to the babies' expressions; the rest of the time, they reacted in the opposite manner. The researchers then held out a hand and requested some food. The children who were at least 18 months old passed over a food that the investigator liked, whereas the younger toddlers were inconsistent with which food they shared. The results of this study indicate that at around the age of 18 months, toddlers begin to be capable of recognizing someone else's perspective.[76]

CHAPTER 7

Enhancing Development With Retro Activities: 19 to 24 Months

Enhancing Development With Retro Activities: 19 to 24 Months

Don't worry that your children never listen to you;
worry that they are always watching you.

~ Robert Fulghum

Your toddler will develop and transform in a variety of ways between the ages of 19 and 24 months. His unique little personality will flourish and shine during this time frame, and he will continue to make developmental strides with his motor and language skills. At this age, he will likely exhibit a strong desire to be more independent, and don't be surprised if he starts pushing the limits on a regular basis. During these months, you'll probably begin to hear the words "me" and "mine" more and more frequently. Watch with pride as your toddler masters the ability to follow simple directions and develops a sense of self. His actions and words will keep you smiling as he works to make sense of the world and his experiences.

By understanding and supporting your toddler's learning process, you will make a positive impact on his development. Have fun carrying out the activities included in this chapter with your little one.

Developmental Milestones: 19 to 24 Months

- Knows names of familiar body parts
- Puts 2 words together
- Follows simple directions
- Points to objects and pictures when named
- Is beginning to sort shapes and colors
- Unzips large zipper
- Copies lines and circular strokes while drawing
- Walks up and down stairs with hand held
- Throws a ball
- Kicks a ball
- Stands on toes
- Is beginning to jump
- Is beginning to run[68,69]

Toy Tips: 19 to 24 Months

- Wagon
- Puppets and dolls
- Dress-up clothing
- Play-Doh
- Shape sorters
- Simple inset puzzles
- Ride-on toys
- Musical instruments
- Lift-a-flap board books
- Mini basketball hoop

Toddler Sleep and Naps

You know the signs. Your child is easily frustrated, rubbing his eyes, and possibly even yawning. It's time for a nap! However, your toddler may not cooperate with the idea of naptime, even if he's exhausted and drowsy. Do your best to have a consistent prenap routine.

Be aware of timing of naps and how long your toddler snoozes during naps. Recent research reveals that longer naptimes and naps that start later in the afternoon lead to toddlers' falling asleep later and getting less sleep at night.[77]

According to the American Academy of Pediatrics, children ranging in age from 12 to 24 months should sleep between 11 and 14 hours during a 24-hour period. This includes naps. Be sure to establish a routine for bedtime, such as brushing teeth, reading a brief story, and kissing him goodnight![78]

Drs Laura A. Jana and Jennifer Shu recommend the 4 Bs of bedtime to ensure bedtime success.[79]

- Baths

- Brushing your child's teeth

- Book reading before bedtime

- Bedtime routines that are regular

Developing Skill: Stacks 5 to 7 Blocks

Between 19 and 24 months, your toddler will begin to use his hands and eyes together in a more efficient manner. His improving visual motor skills will make it easier for him to carry out self-care skills such as eating with a spoon and zipping and unzipping a jacket. As he becomes more adept at controlling the small muscles in the hands and fingers, he will enjoy stacking blocks and stringing large beads during play, and he will likely show an increased interest in using a crayon to mark or scribble on paper. But watch out, because he may also be tempted to decorate your walls! The following activities are good for improving eye-hand coordination.

Truth Be Told

Around this age, toddlers typically hold a crayon or utensil using the fingers and the tip of the thumb, with the thumb turned toward the paper. This is called a *pronated grasp.*

Activities to Improve Visual-Motor Skills

Activity 1: Colander Adventure

All you will need for this activity is a handful of colorful pipe cleaners and a plastic kitchen colander. Fold the tips of the pipe cleaners over and twist them tightly so there will be no sharp ends. Now show your little one how to thread each pipe cleaner through the colander holes, and turn him loose! This is an ideal activity for promoting independent play.

Activity 2: Poker Face

Trace the outline of 10 poker chips on a medium-sized piece of foam board. The circles can form the outline of a simple shape, such as a circle or triangle. You can also design a "poker face." Use a marker to color the various circles to match the colors of the poker chips. For example, if the poker chips are red, blue, and black, the circles should correspond. Show your toddler how to place each poker chip on top of the matching circle. This requires precision and might be slightly challenging for him, so feel free to provide a bit of assistance as needed. You may want to add small pieces of Velcro to the board and chips so that the poker chips will stay in place.

Activity 3: Spool Stack

Recycle your empty wooden or plastic thread spools for a stacking activity that your toddler will enjoy. Cut strips of colorful paper to fit outside each spool, and glue or tape the paper around each one. Once the spools are decorated, show your child how to build a tower or simple pyramid with the spools. Stacking the spools is good for his focus and concentration. For even more entertainment, encourage him to knock the tower down. Time to start all over!

Activity 4: Feeding Frenzy

For this activity, you'll need to collect various sizes of plastic lids that are approximately 2 inches in diameter. You will also need an empty plastic wet-wipe container. Use a permanent marker to draw two eyes just above the opening in the top of the wipe container. (The opening will be the mouth.) Encourage your toddler to "feed" the lids through the opening. Give the container a silly name, and make your child laugh by saying, "Mr. Mouth is hungry. Can you feed him? He says, 'Yummy, yummy in my tummy!'"

Activity 5: Cotton Art

Take an empty egg carton and put several colors of water-color paint into different sections in the carton. Give your child 3 or 4 clean round or square cotton pads. Show him how to hold the cotton pad using his thumb and fingers and dip it into one of the paint colors. Now have him paint a picture by dabbing a piece of paper with the cotton. He should use a fresh cotton pad when he switches colors. Be sure to praise your little artist when he finishes his master-piece. For more information on praise, refer to Chapter 3.

Rub-a-Dub-Dub

Rub a dub dub,

Three men in a tub,

And who do you think they be?

The butcher,

The baker,

The candlestick maker,

Turn them out, knaves all three!

Developing Skill: Squats While Playing

Leg strength is important for standing, walking, balancing, transitioning from sitting to standing, and squatting while playing. Your toddler also needs strong legs for running, jumping, and climbing, so be sure to provide plenty of opportunities for him to move about freely, climb, and be physically active. The following activities strengthen the legs and promote balance and stability.

Activities to Improve Balance and Stability

Activity 1: Stepping It Up!

Have your toddler crawl up several stairs to retrieve a desirable item and bring the item back down to you. This is great for his motor planning skills. You can also hold his hand and walk him up and down the stairs slowly. Sing a fun song together as you climb, "Up, up, up we go," and descend, "Down, down, down we go." When you reach the bottom step, encourage your toddler to jump from the bottom step to the floor as the grand finale. If needed, prompt him to bend his knees right before he jumps. This will make jumping easier.

Activity 2: Going Down, Down, Down!

When your child is holding onto the edge of a sofa or ottoman, place 2 or 3 interesting toys on the floor just within reach. Ask your toddler to retrieve a toy and place it on the sofa. As he squats down and back up, he will be strengthening his legs, which enhances his balance and stability.

Activity 3: Frog Hop

Pretend you are a frog and jump up and down as you sing this song. Encourage your toddler to imitate your actions.

Five Green Speckled Frogs

Five green speckled frogs
sat on a speckled log,
Eating some most delicious bugs.
Yum, yum!
One jumped into the pool
where it was nice and cool,
Then there were four green
speckled frogs.
Glub, glub!

Activity 4: Tunnel Time

Use a pop-up laundry basket as a play tunnel for your toddler to crawl through. Navigating through the tunnel will develop his *gross motor skills,* such as control of the movement of his arms and legs. This activity is also good for motor planning and increasing body awareness. To ensure safety, check the tunnel frequently to be sure the fabric is in good shape and the wires are fully enclosed.

Preventing Injuries From Toys

Injuries from toys tend to be minor cuts, scratches, or bruises, but toys can cause severe injury or possibly death if used in the wrong way.

Here are tips to help you choose safe and appropriate toys for your child.

1. Read the label. Warning labels give important information about how to use a toy and the ages for which the toy is safe. Be sure to show your child how to use the toy the right way. Even better, follow the recommended ages as noted on the package.

2. Think LARGE. Make sure all toys and parts are larger than your child's mouth to prevent choking.

3. Avoid toys that shoot objects into the air. They can cause serious eye injuries or choking.

4. Avoid toys that are loud to prevent damage to your child's hearing.

5. Look for stuffed toys that are well made. Make sure all the parts are on tight and seams and edges are secure. It should also be machine washable. Take off any loose ribbons or strings to avoid strangulation. Avoid toys that contain small beanlike pellets or stuffing that can cause choking or suffocation if swallowed.

6. Buy plastic toys that are sturdy. Toys made from thin plastic may break easily.

7. Avoid toys with toxic materials that could cause poisoning. Make sure the label says "nontoxic."

8. Avoid hobby kits and chemistry sets for any child younger than 12 years. They can cause fires or explosions and may contain dangerous chemicals. Make sure your older child knows how to safely handle these kinds of toys.

9. Electric toys should bear the Underwriters Laboratories (UL) logo. Check the label to be sure.[80]

Activity 5: Shopping Trip

Place several small toys in several places on the floor. Give your toddler a small basket and ask him to gather all the toys, place them in the basket, and bring them to you. Squatting down to get the toys and standing back up will strengthen his leg muscles and develop his balance.

Developing Skill: Learning Body Parts

Your toddler continues to make strides with his cognitive skills. He is constantly learning new concepts and words, and he is at the age at which he is learning how to point to and name the various parts of his body. Here are 5 fun activities that will help your little one learn his body parts.

Activities for Learning About the Body

Activity 1: Name That Body Part

During dressing, talk about your child's various body parts. For example, "Let's pull the shirt over your head. Now put your arm through the sleeve. Where is your arm? There it is!" It's also a good idea to teach your toddler about the function of each body part during this activity, such as, "You see with your eyes, you lick with your tongue, and you hear with your ears." Remember, he's always learning, so never pass up a teaching opportunity.

Activity 2: Sponge Bath

During bath time, encourage your toddler to look at each body part and name it while washing it with a sponge or washcloth. For example, while watching his neck, say, "We're cleaning your…." Pause and wait for him to name the body part, and prompt him if he needs some help. This is a natural way to teach him the parts of the body. Rubbing the body part with the washcloth or sponge provides sensory input, which increases body awareness.

Activity 3: Me Puzzle

Take a full-body photo of your child and print it on a large piece of card stock. Cut the image into a several different pieces—torso, head, arms, legs. If you have sticky laminating film, use it to cover the card stock. This will make the puzzle sturdy so it will last longer. Your toddler will enjoy putting the puzzle together, and he will be increasing the awareness of his body parts while also strengthening his *visual perceptual skills.*

Activity 4: My Body Game

Have your toddler cover his eyes with his hands. Use your finger to touch him on his arm, hand, or leg and ask him where he was touched. Start by using more pressure and slightly rubbing the area and, as he catches on, gradually reduce the amount of pressure. Now switch places with him and have him try the game on you.

Activity 5: Paper Plate Faces

For this activity, you will need a plain white paper plate and some Play-Doh. Show your child how to form the dough into eyes, ears, nose, and mouth. Encourage him to orient each body part to make a face on the paper plate. Once he masters the simple face, have him progress to more challenging parts such as hair and eyebrows.

Developing Skill: Sense of Self Is Developing

At around 2 years old, toddlers begin to develop a sense of self, or self-concept. They begin to see themselves as separate beings from their parents with intentions of their own. It is around this time that your little one starts to recognize himself in a mirror and begins using the terms "I," "me," and "mine."

In a classic study known as the "rouge test," moms put a small amount of rouge on their children's noses. The toddlers were then positioned in front of a mirror. The children who were younger than 15 months looked in the mirror and did not see the red color on their nose. The youngsters between 15 and 24 months pointed to the rouge or attempted to wipe it off because they realized the reflection was their own, a sign of self-awareness![81]

Interestingly, a child's self-concept is closely linked to body awareness, which is knowing the body's location in space, its size, and how it moves. A 2007 study found that children between 18 and 22 months of age were not yet aware of their body size. For example, the young children in the study attempted to try on tiny doll clothing, fit through a small door, and use doll-sized furniture that was too small for them. The toddlers seemed unaware of their body size until they were closer to 26 months of age, and at that time, their body awareness improved. This is also the age range in which young children typically begin to test limits.[82]

Truth Be Told

Reading aloud to your toddler will expand his vocabulary and promote literacy.[83]

Activities to Promote Self-awareness

Activity 1: Body Talk

Have some fun with your little one while increasing his body awareness. Position him in front of a mirror and have him point to his different body parts. Call them out slowly at first and increase your pace as he catches on. Add a tune and sing the body parts for even more entertainment.

Activity 2: Watch Me Grow

Mount a chart on the wall to measure your toddler's height every 6 months. Have him stand up tall while you make a line on the chart just above the top of his head. Then have him turn around to see the mark. He will be excited to see how much he's grown! Be sure to include a date beside each mark. One day, the chart will be a special keepsake.

Activity 3: Floor Flapping

Have your child lie on a clean floor with his arms to his sides. Instruct him to raise his arms at the same time he moves his legs apart and lower his arms as he brings his legs back together. You may need to demonstrate the movement. At first, have him carry out the activity on a smooth surface, such as a hardwood floor; then have him try it on a carpeted surface. Ask him if the two experiences felt different. This activity is a fun sensory experience, and it increases body awareness.

Activity 4: My Very Own Body

Have your child lie down on a large piece of butcher paper and use a crayon to trace around his body. Cut along the outline using a pair of scissors. Ask your toddler where his various body parts are located (eyes, nose, hair, belly button) and as he shows you, draw them on the paper. He may need a little help to get it right, but that's what you're there for!

Activity 5: Copycat

Assume a position in which one of your body parts is touching another body part, and encourage your toddler to copy you. Examples include ear to shoulder, elbow to knee, hands on hips, and crossing legs. Get creative and silly with the positions!

Truth Be Told

When our muscles and joints tighten, stretch, and move, sensations are sent to our brain. These sensations are called "proprioceptive input." The brain interprets the sensations, and this is how we know how we move and where our bodies are in space. This is called *"proprioception,"* and it plays an important role in body awareness. For example, when you close your eyes and hold your arms out to the side, it is the proprioceptive input that lets you know where your arms are located without using your vision.

Little Boy Blue

Little boy blue,

Come blow your horn.

The sheep's in the meadow,

The cow's in the corn.

Where's the little boy who looks after the sheep?

Under the haystack,

Fast asleep.

Will you wake him?

No, not I,

For if I do,

He's sure to cry.

Developing Skill: Problem-solving

As your toddler interacts with the environment, he is constantly gaining problem-solving experience and developing an understanding of the world. As he works to achieve goals, he will learn how to reach solutions through trial and error. There may be times when he struggles to come up with a solution, and a meltdown follows. However, don't be too quick to rush in and save the day. He may only need a bit of encouragement or a prompt to point him in the right direction. When your child solves problems independently, his confidence will grow. The ability to solve problems is an important life skill, so cheer your toddler on one solution at a time!

Activities to Improve Problem-solving Skills

Activity 1: Measuring Up

Plastic measuring cups make a fun *nesting* toy for toddler play. Your child will need to learn how to discriminate the different sizes of the cups to be able to nest them correctly. This is typically done through trial and error, but you can provide some guidance by showing him how to line them up from smallest to largest. This entertaining activity is great for developing problem-solving skills.

Activity 2: Just the Same

For this activity, you will need a variety of everyday objects, such as plastic utensils, socks, and plastic cups that are different sizes, shapes, and colors. Make sure that you have more than one of each item. Show your child one of the objects and ask him to find an item just like yours. Once he's made his selection, ask him to tell you how the items are similar and how they are different. This activity addresses memory and following directions.

Activity 3: Listen to the Story

Read a book aloud and ask your toddler simple questions about the story—for example, "Was the dog black or white? Was it a cloudy or sunny day?" If there are animals in the book, make the appropriate animal noise and ask your child to point to the animal that makes that sound. This game exercises his listening skills.

Truth Be Told

When a father regularly reads to his child, the child is more likely to be academically successful[84] and to have improved emotional and social health.[85]

Activity 4: Pudding Art

Pour some pudding on a cookie sheet and show your child how to imitate horizontal, vertical, and circular lines by using his index finger. Provide a little guidance at first if he's having difficulty. It's also a good idea to verbalize what you are doing when you demonstrate by saying, "Line down, line across, and circle around." Children typically imitate strokes first and then form them independently. Before you know it, your little one will be writing letters!

Activity 5: Silly Sounds

Use the recorder on your phone to tape a variety of sounds that your child will recognize, such as stomping, clapping, or humming. Play the sounds for him one at a time and encourage him to guess what made the noise. He may need a clue or two, but that's OK!

Toddler Temper Tantrums

As a parent, you may be able to sense that your child is going to throw a fit before it ever even happens, but not always. When your toddler throws himself on the floor and has a full-blown tantrum, do your best to stay calm. As overwhelming as tantrums can be, they are a typical behavior to expect from a young child. Why? During the toddler years, frustrations are commonplace because of limited language and immature motor skills—and when a child this young experiences frustration, he is unable to communicate his feelings with words and has difficulty controlling his emotions. Thus, the frustration comes out as a tantrum.

Research reveals that tantrums have distinguishable patterns that may include screaming, kicking, crying, and whining, with anger and sadness occurring simultaneously. Considering this, parents should ignore the tantrum until the anger wanes, while making sure the child is safe. At that point, it's fine to step in and provide comfort.[86] If the situation does not allow you to ignore the tantrum, speak calmly to your child, acknowledge his feelings, and encourage him to use his words to express himself. Here are several additional tips for dealing with temper tantrums.

- Do your best to understand your child's situation. Is he frustrated, tired, or hungry? If these needs have been met but the tantrum continues, it's fine to try to distract him.
- If you see that a frustrating situation is forthcoming, help your toddler use his words. If he is not speaking yet, show him how to use basic signs to communicate.
- Watch your child carefully and be aware of his expressions and body language. When he successfully navigates a challenging situation without throwing a fit, praise him for using these skills. Remember, be specific with your praise: "I like how you used your words to ask for help." Take advantage of those teachable moments.
- Offer choices whenever possible. For example, ask him, "Do you want milk or juice? Would you like to wear your green shirt or the yellow one? Do you want to play outside or inside this afternoon?"
- After the tantrum passes and your child settles down, validate his feelings.

CHAPTER 8

Enhancing Development With Retro Activities: 25 to 30 Months

CHAPTER 8

Enhancing Development With Retro Activities: 25 to 30 Months

*Children are apt to live up to
what you believe of them.*

~ Lady Bird Johnson

At this phase of her development, your toddler is talking more, and she is learning how to match objects, shapes, and colors. You may even notice that she has developed a sense of humor, so keep your ears open for laughter! At this age, your little one likely enjoys interacting with peers of the same age, but don't expect sharing to come easily just yet. This takes time. One of the best ways to teach your child how to share is to model sharing behavior. For instance, if you are eating raisins as a snack (one raisin at a time), offer her several. Be sure to point out that you are sharing with her to help her understand the concept.

Remember to limit the use of technology and smartphones when you are with your toddler. These gadgets will prevent you from spending quality time with your little one. Pay attention when the two of you are interacting and treasure the time you spend together. The no-technology rule is especially important when you are dining together as a family. At this age, your toddler can drink from a cup and feed herself with little spilling, so mealtime won't be as messy as it used to be. That's good news!

Developmental Milestones: 25 to 30 Months

- Pulls toy when walking
- Climbs on furniture
- May throw a tantrum when frustrated
- Engages in defiant behavior
- Follows simple instructions
- Refers to self by name
- Ascends and descends stairs while holding rail
- Puts on socks
- Opens a jar

- Speaks using simple phrases
- Follows directions related to *prepositions* (in, behind)
- Strings large beads
- Opens a door by turning the doorknob[68,69]

Toy Tips: 25 to 30 Months

- Age-appropriate construction activity set
- Toy kitchen set
- Finger paints
- Toy wheelbarrow
- Blow toys
- Wooden pounding bench
- Stuffed animals
- Sidewalk chalk
- Wooden A-B-C and 1-2-3 blocks
- Puzzles of 4 to 5 pieces
- Books

Help! My Toddler Is a Picky Eater

If your child is fussy about what she eats, rest assured. Picky eating is quite common during the toddler years. Your little one may refuse to eat a certain food item one day and then accept it the next. Her appetite and preferences will likely vary, but that is to be expected at this age. Her limited menu may be frustrating for you—but remember, when you are stressed, your child will sense your anxiety. So try to stay calm and avoid pressuring her to eat a food item that she refuses. Take it slowly and introduce new foods one at a time. Try exposing her to new foods gradually. For example, start by putting one serving on her plate, and encourage her to look at it, touch it, smell it, and explore it, but don't force her to eat it. Repeat this at subsequent meals, and eventually, she may dig in on her own!

You can also try giving new foods fun names. In a fairly recent experiment, when researchers called food by different names, such as "Power Punch Broccoli" and "X-Ray Vision Carrots," the children in the study were more likely to eat the broccoli and carrots.[87]

Be a good role model by eating balanced healthy meals. Do your best to offer several nutritious options at mealtime, and make sure that the foods on your child's plate are cut into small pieces that she can easily chew. Always keep a close eye on your child while she's eating. To decrease the risk of choking, the American Academy of Pediatrics (AAP) recommends not introducing the following foods until 4 years of age: raw carrots, raw celery, whole grapes, raw cherries with pits, nuts, hard candy, and large pieces of hot dog. Check out *The Picky Eater Project: 6 Weeks to Happier, Healthier Family Mealtimes* by Natalie Digate Muth, MD, MPH, RDN, FAAP, and Sally Sampson, Founder, ChopChopKids (AAP, 2017).

Developing Skill: Turns Individual Pages in a Book

During this phase of toddlerhood, your child is moving her fingers with increasing control. Her improved hand skills will allow her to explore and manipulate small items with more precision. For example, she will be able to turn one page at a time, line 3 to 4 blocks in a row to make a pretend train, and put simple puzzles together. Here are some fun activities to promote the development of your child's hand skills.

Truth Be Told

When looking at picture books with your toddler, point to characters and encourage her to talk about how the characters feel. This will help your child develop empathy.[88]

Activities for Hand Skills

Activity 1: Tug-a-Tug

Hold one end of a popsicle stick with your thumb and index finger and show your child how to do the same at the other end. It may be helpful to place a small sticker on either side of the stick to mark where the thumb and index finger should be positioned. Once you both have a firm grip on the stick, play tug-of-war! Pull gently, keeping in mind that the small muscles in your child's thumb and fingers are still gaining strength.

Activity 2: Leaf Art

Take your toddler outside and have her remove a good-sized leaf from a tree or shrub. Use several strips of tape to secure the leaf onto a piece of paper, and place another piece of paper on top of the leaf. Have your child color on the paper over the leaf with a crayon. She may want to use more than one color. It's her choice! Be sure that she uses her nondominant hand to

hold the paper in place, prompting her as needed. As your little one colors, the outline of the leaf will gradually show up. Be sure to display the final project for the entire family to see.

Activity 3: Easel Work

Have your child use a vertical surface such as an easel when coloring, drawing, or painting. This will put the paper in her line of vision, strengthen her shoulders, exercise the small muscles in her hands, and facilitate a nice extended wrist position when holding the writing utensil. Working on a vertical surface also promotes good posture. An added bonus is that artistic opportunities promote creativity!

Activity 4: It's a Wrap

Wrap several of your toddler's small toys or stuffed animals with tissue or wrapping paper and have a pretend birthday party. She will get a kick out of unwrapping the items, and pinching and pulling the wrapping paper will be good for her *fine motor skills* and her *bilateral skills.* Have her examine the package before she opens it, and see if she can guess what is inside. She may also want to help you wrap an item for someone else to open!

Activity 5: Stringing Straws

Take 3 or 4 different colors of plastic straws and have your child snip them into small strips with safe child-sized scissors. She may need prompts to hold the scissors correctly.

Have her string the straws onto a 6-inch piece of yarn. If she has a hard time threading the yarn through the small holes, take a short piece of scotch tape and wrap it tightly around the tip of the yarn so that it will stay straight. This should make threading easier. Just tie the finished product around her wrist, and she will have her very own bracelet. She may even want to make several more to give to her friends!

Five Little Ducks

Five little ducks
Went out one day,
Over the hill and far away.
Mother Duck said,
"Quack, quack, quack, quack."
But only four little ducks came back.

Four little ducks
Went out one day,
Over the hill and far away.
Mother Duck said,
"Quack, quack, quack, quack."
But only three little ducks came back.

Three little ducks
Went out one day,
Over the hill and far away.
Mother Duck said,
"Quack, quack, quack, quack."
But only two little ducks came back.

Two little ducks
Went out one day,
Over the hill and far away.
Mother Duck said,
"Quack, quack, quack, quack."
But only one little duck came back.

One little duck
Went out one day,
Over the hill and far away.
Mother Duck said,
"Quack, quack, quack, quack."
But none of the five little ducks came back.

Sad Mother Duck
Went out one day,
Over the hill and far away.
Sad Mother Duck said,
"Quack, quack, quack, quack."
And all of the five little ducks came back!

Developing Skill: Jumps Forward

It's likely that your toddler can now jump forward several inches. Jumping is a fun physical activity that strengthens the legs and promotes balance and body awareness. Children often run and jump during active play, which strengthens the large muscles and improves endurance. The following activities will help your toddler further develop her *gross motor skills,* which will help with running and jumping.

Activities for Jumping and Gross Motor Skills

Activity 1: Crab Walk

Sit on the floor and place your hands behind you. Use your arms to lift your bottom off the ground. Use your hands and feet to propel yourself forward like a crab. Encourage your child to imitate you. Holding herself up and moving forward will be difficult at first, but as she gains strength and coordination, it will be less challenging. Once she gets the hang of it, race her across the room!

Activity 2: Shape Jump

Use masking or painter's tape to form 3 or 4 basic shapes on the floor several inches apart. Have your child jump from one shape to the next while calling out the name of the shape that she lands on. Demonstrate the activity for her first so that she understands the game. She will gain leg strength and endurance while learning the various shapes. As she gains more skill and confidence, gradually increase the distance between the shapes.

Activity 3: Stomp on the Bubble Wrap

Secure a long strip of plastic Bubble Wrap on the floor by using several strips of masking tape. Encourage your little one to stomp on the Bubble Wrap to make it pop. Show her how to pop the bubbles with her toes, her heel, and her entire foot. Jumping up and down on the Bubble Wrap is another way to make it pop, but if she tries this, be sure to hold her hand to ensure that she doesn't slip and fall.

Activity 4: Step and Squeak

For this activity, you will need one or two dog toys that squeak when squeezed. Place the squeak toys on the floor in front of your toddler and show her how to step on them one at a time to make them squeak. This activity can be made more challenging by having her use alternate feet when stepping. If the toys move when she steps on them, secure them in place with masking tape.

Activity 5: Jump Ball!

Tie a beach ball or Mylar balloon to a long piece of string and use two strips of painter's tape to attach the string to the ceiling. Position the ball or balloon just out of your child's reach so that she has to jump to touch it.

Encourage her to jump up and bat the ball with her hand. Stand close by so you can catch her if she loses her balance. Count out loud every time she successfully hits the ball. This will help her learn her numbers, and this activity is a fun way to get active while developing eye-hand coordination. Instead of counting, another option is to sing a counting song or recite a nursery rhyme during this activity. "Five Little Monkeys" is a fun option.

Five Little Monkeys

Five little monkeys jumping on the bed,
One fell off and bumped his head.
Mama called the doctor, and the doctor said,
"No more monkeys jumping on the bed!"

Developing Skill: Matches Simple Shapes

As your child continues to grow and gain skills, you will notice advances in her thinking. She will understand concepts such as "same" and "different" and begin to organize visual information to make sense of it. *Visual discrimination* is the ability to see slight differences in objects or pictures, a skill that is the foundation of shape recognition. It is also an important preliteracy skill. The following activities are entertaining ways to practice shape matching and recognition and to sharpen *visual discrimination* skills.

Activities for Learning Shapes

Activity 1: Gel Bag Fun!

In a large plastic freezer bag, place some inexpensive hair gel, several drops of food coloring, and a bit of glitter. Seal the bag and make sure that there are no air pockets inside. Secure the seal by using a strip of duct tape. Smooth out the bag on a flat surface and form a shape using your index finger while your child watches. After you "erase" your shape, tell your little one it's her turn! She will enjoy imitating a variety of basic shapes and strokes.

Activity 2: Magic Wand Writing

Remove the cardboard tube from a wire pants hanger and cut it to 4 inches in length. To make the magic wand, cut 5 or 6 strips of crepe paper, each 18 to 24 inches long, and tape them to the end of the tube. If you prefer, you can use colorful strands of yarn instead of crepe paper. Show your toddler how to move the magic wand through the air to form shapes or patterns. This activity will help your child learn various shapes, and the large arm movement will help her remember how to form each one. Provide verbal prompts such as, "Draw a circle in the air. Move your arm around and around!"

Activity 3: Rainbow Shapes

For this fun activity, you will need at least 3 different colors of sidewalk chalk. Start by showing your child a picture of a rainbow; then you can draw the outline of a basic shape on the sidewalk or a piece of black construction paper. Next, show her how to trace the outer edge of the shape with one color. Have her trace the shape again with a different color and then another. She will have fun making rainbow circles, squares, triangles, and rectangles!

Activity 4: Touch-and-Feel Shapes

Help your toddler form a circle on a small sheet of card stock with white craft glue, then have her sprinkle glitter over the wet glue. Encourage her to "pinch" the glitter by using her thumb and index finger before sprinkling it. She can also make cards with other shapes, such as a triangle, an oval, and a square. After the cards dry, your child can trace the shapes with her fingertip for a great "sensory" learning experience. If you don't have any glitter, use colored sugar or sand.

Activity 5: String Shapes

Have your toddler make a shape poster by gluing colorful pieces of yarn or string on a large poster board to form different shapes. As she is making the shapes, talk about how they are formed. For example, "Look, the square has four corners…one, two, three, four!" Once the glue dries, she will enjoy tracing the various shapes with her fingertip.

Sensory Play!

If your toddler enjoys getting messy while playing, that is just fine. In fact, believe it or not, messy play is a good thing! Why? It's a sensory experience that provides opportunities for your child to learn to tolerate different sensations and textures. Examples of messy play are finding small toys hidden in a sand box, squeezing and manipulating Play-Doh, finger painting, and playing in shaving cream. Because toddlers may put their hands in their mouths, supervise your child closely during these activities— and remember, there will be plenty of time to clean up later!

Developing Skill: Understands and Follows 2- or 3-Step Directions

The ability to follow directions is an important life skill, and you may have noticed that at this age your toddler is beginning to follow multistep directions. This means that your child listens to your directives and holds those directives in her memory while carrying out actions. For example, you may tell her to go to the closet and get her coat. While walking to the closet, she has to remember not only where she is going but also that she is supposed to retrieve the coat. This can be challenging, so don't hesitate to provide reminders as needed. Start with simple instructions and move to more complex directions. Here are some great tips to work on following directions.

Activities for Following 2- to 3-Step Directions

Activity 1: Let's Get Physical

Instruct your toddler, "Jump up and down and stomp one foot." Once she completes that successfully, add another movement: "Jump up and down, stomp one foot, and scratch your head." Additional movement options include marching by lifting the knees high in the air, turning in a circle, and doing a silly dance. Be sure to clap your hands and cheer when your child completes the sequence successfully.

Activity 2: Gym Tape Maze

Use colorful gym tape to create a simple maze on the floor. Walk through the maze and encourage your child to follow you. After you both have walked the maze several times, have her go through it all by herself. Give her clear directions for how to navigate the maze before she starts. When she reaches the end, be sure to tell her, "Good job!"

Activity 3: Indoor Do-it-yourself Croquet

For this game, you will need different colored sheets of sturdy construction paper, scissors, masking tape, an empty gift-wrap tube, and a ping-pong ball or mini tennis ball. Cut 4 or 5 strips of construction paper, each of a different color. The strips should be 3 inches wide by 10 inches long. Use each strip to make an arch by securing the ends of the strips to the ground with masking tape. The empty gift-wrap tube will serve as the mallet. Show your child how to knock the ball through an arch by using the tube. Once she has the hang of it, give her some instructions to follow—for example, "Hit the ball through the yellow arch, the blue arch, and then the red arch."

Truth Be Told

Play provides children with opportunities to develop imagination and creativity.[89]

Activity 4: Shake, Shake, Shake!

To make a shaker, just put a handful of colorful buttons inside a small water bottle and use nontoxic glue to secure the top in place. Be sure to make 2—you'll need 1 for you and 1 for your child. Tell your little one to listen carefully as you use the shaker to make a simple musical pattern, and then have her imitate you. She may need to hear the pattern several times before she can successfully imitate the sound.

Activity 5: Scavenger Hunt

Use a digital camera to take photos of different locations in the house where you plan to hide objects for a scavenger hunt: under a throw pillow on the sofa, behind a chair, under a blanket, in the bathtub. Objects to hunt could be a stuffed animal, a small toy, or a large ball. Tell your toddler that you hid some objects and explain how she can use the photos to find the items. She made need a little guidance at first, but in no time, she'll be locating the surprises all by herself!

The Importance of Manners

As your toddler continues to grow and develop, you will notice that she is becoming more social and using social language, such as "thank you" and "please." These common courtesies are important, as they show respect for and appreciation of others. Parents can help their children learn good manners by modeling these social niceties. In fact, having good manners is important for one's future success. A 2015 study revealed that young children with strong social skills are more likely to be well-educated and work full-time as adults.[90]

Developing Skill: Engages in Pretend Play

You may have noticed your toddler beginning to engage in pretend or make-believe play. No doubt, she will have fun as she acts out her thoughts and ideas. *Pretend play* provides opportunities for your little one to express her emotions, practice different skills, and use objects in a creative way. Pretending is also great for problem-solving and for developing social and communication skills. Keep in mind that unstructured play encourages *pretend play* and use of the imagination.

On Top of Spaghetti

On top of spaghetti,
All covered with cheese,
I lost my poor meatball
When somebody sneezed.

It rolled off the table,
And onto the floor,
And then my poor meatball
Rolled out of the door.

It rolled into the garden,
And under a bush,
And then my poor meatball
Was nothing but mush.

The mush was as tasty
As tasty could be,
And then the next summer
It grew into a tree.

The tree was all covered,
All covered with moss,
And on it grew meatballs
And tomato sauce.

So if you eat spaghetti,
All covered with cheese,
Hold on to your meatball
Whenever you sneeze.

Activities for Pretending

The following activities promote *pretend play* and are loads of fun!

Activity 1: Pretend Puppet Play

Help your toddler create several of her very own puppets for a fun puppet show. First, help her choose a theme for the show. For example, ask her if she wants the show to be about animals, dinosaurs, or her favorite characters from a book. You'll need several small paper bags, glue, child-safe scissors, and construction paper. Cut out a variety of eyes, noses, mouths, and ears for your child to choose from. Position the bag flat on a table with the flap on top and help her decorate the puppet. When you glue the pieces in place, encourage your toddler to help you squeeze the glue. She will enjoy helping out. Give the glue plenty of time to dry. Now for the fun part! Show her how to slip her hand inside and open and close the mouth. Once she has that down, she can put on a puppet show for you. Encourage her to use her imagination!

Activity 2: Sail On!

Your toddler can pretend she is sailing the seas! All she needs for this activity is a laundry basket. However, if you want to add a sail, an empty gift-wrap tube with a small washcloth attached to it will work just fine. Tell your little one to hop aboard the boat, and she can use her imagination to sail the day away! You may want to occasionally give her a push to propel the boat forward. She will surely get a kick out of that. You can even teach her the following sailing song to sing during the activity.

Sailing, Sailing

Sailing, sailing,
Over the bounding main,
For many a stormy wind shall blow
'Til (insert your child's name here)
comes home again.

Activity 3: Superhero Cape

Use a colorful piece of cloth or old towel as a superhero cape for your little one. Adhesive-backed Velcro works well to secure the cape in the front. All your toddler needs to do is stretch those arms out and pretend to fly across the sky! You can also show her how to position herself on her stomach with her arms outstretched in

front of her and legs extended. Ask her to lift her arms and legs off of the floor for a few seconds without bending her elbows or knees. This is challenging, but it's good for strengthening the core muscles. No doubt, your little one will have fun pretending to be a powerful and helpful superhero!

Activity 4: Playing Chef

Provide your child with plastic pots, pans, cups, dishes, and utensils. Encourage her to pretend to be a chef by cooking a gourmet meal. Short pieces of yellow yarn can be served as pasta. You can also cut fun foods out of different pieces of felt, such as a fried egg, a slice of cheese, and a piece of bread. Large plastic lids make wonderful pancakes! Show your little one how to use a spatula to flip the pancake. This will take some practice. The flipping motion is good for motor skills and coordination.

My Helping Chart

A helping chart is a wonderful way to motivate your toddler to pitch in with simple daily tasks. Use a digital camera and take photos to represent the various tasks that you want your little one to complete. For example, you might use a photo of a bed to represent making the bed or a photo of the clothes hamper for putting dirty laundry where it belongs. Post the chart in a spot your child can reach and have her put a sticker on each photo as she successfully completes a task. If you laminate the chart, it will last quite a while.

Activity 5: Household Helper

Your toddler loves to be a helper, and helping around the house is a wonderful way to learn a variety of lessons. Have her assist you with simple household tasks such as making her bed, sweeping the floors, stirring safe ingredients, and doing light house cleaning. If you are preparing a meal, give your child an opportunity to lend a helping hand. She will enjoy stirring ingredients and rolling dough, and you can even have her help you with measurements. When the meal is complete, join her at the sink and show her how to wash and dry the dishes and utensils that aren't sharp or breakable.

When it's cleaning time, let your toddler join in the fun. Show her how to pick up her toys and put them in the proper place. As she watches you work around the house dusting, mopping floors, and wiping surfaces, she can even pretend to be Mommy or Daddy as she dusts with her very own dust mop. No doubt, your child's self-esteem and confidence will grow when she realizes that she is truly helping.

My Very Own Dust Mop

You will need

- **Yarn**

- **1 Straw**

- **Colorful masking or duct tape**

- **Scissors**

Wrap the yarn around the palm of your hand approximately 75 times. Remove your hand while holding one end of the loops with your fingers. Use a piece of yarn and tie it tightly around the loops, then cut the loops at the opposite end with sharp scissors. Place the straw over the yarn loop where you tied the knot and fold it around the loops. Wrap the tape around the folded straw to make the handle of the dust mop. Tie another piece of yarn around the yarn just below the handle you just made. Voilà! It's cleaning time!

CHAPTER 9

Enhancing Development With Retro Activities: 31 to 36 Months

CHAPTER 9

Enhancing Development With Retro Activities: 31 to 36 Months

Parents need to fill a child's bucket of self-esteem so high that the rest of the world can't poke enough holes to drain it dry.

~ Alvin Price

Can you believe how quickly time has passed? As your toddler has explored and followed his interests, he has learned so much about the world around him. However, there is still so much learning ahead! In the coming months, your child's vocabulary will continue to expand, he'll learn how to snip with child-safe scissors, and he will begin to understand concepts, such as "now" and "later." As your toddler becomes more independent, it is important not to be overprotective. Give him ample opportunities to make choices for himself, and don't be afraid to let him fail now and then. Remember, he will learn how to persevere by facing challenges and dealing with occasional failures. His path to independence may not always be easy, but that's OK.

This chapter provides a variety of stimulating play activities that will enrich your toddler's development. As you incorporate the following activities into your everyday routines, you and your child will have lots of fun together. Enjoy these special times, because time passes quickly, and it won't be long before your little one is a preschooler!

Developmental Milestones: 31 to 36 Months

- Uses pronouns ("I," "you," "mine")
- Tells stories
- Engages in *pretend play*
- Imitates a cross and circle while drawing
- Copies a square
- Stacks 5 or more blocks

- Snips with child-sized safe scissors
- Turns the pages of a book one at a time
- Alternates feet on stairs
- Climbs a small ladder
- Pedals a tricycle
- Says name, age, and sex
- Understands words such as "on," "in," "over"[68,69]

Toy Tips: 31 to 36 Months

- Bubbles
- Tongs
- Small plastic people
- Small plastic animals
- Doll
- Doll house
- Tactile balls of large sizes
- Number and alphabet puzzles
- Lacing cards
- Books with words and pictures
- Tricycle

Developing Skill: Dresses Self With Little to No Help

Your 3-year-old is likely undressing and dressing with minimal assistance. When it comes to self-help skills, practice makes perfect, so encourage his independence by setting his clothing out or make sure the clothes are within reach in a low drawer or on a low shelf. If your little one needs prompts when dressing, provide simple, clear verbal instructions and demonstrate a skill if necessary. Socks and shoes may be challenging, so provide assistance as needed. Take the opportunity to praise him when he takes the initiative to be more independent with his self-help skills. This will boost his confidence and promote success.

Activities for Dressing Skills

Activity 1: Clothespins

Show your toddler how to squeeze and place clothespins on a sturdy strip of cardboard. This will strengthen the tiny muscles in the thumb and fingers and is a wonderful activity for improving eye-hand coordination. If you have several different colors of clothespins, make the activity more challenging by wrapping corresponding colors of tape strips around the cardboard strip, then encouraging your little one to match the colors.

Learning to Color Within the Lines

Does your child have difficulty staying within the lines when coloring a picture? Coloring inside the lines is challenging to master. This technique might be helpful: use clear school glue and outline the edges of a simple coloring picture. Once the glue dries, have your child color the picture. When his crayon bumps against the dried glue, this will give him a sensory cue that he has reached the line. Start with thick glue lines and gradually reduce the thickness as your child's skills improve.

Activity 2: Break Those Crayons!

Early on, your toddler will have limited control when coloring with crayons. He will start with an immature fisted grasp to hold the crayon, and he will likely move his whole arm back and forth to scribble on a piece of paper. Gradually, his grasp will mature, and he'll begin to use more wrist and finger movements when making marks. You can promote a better grasp on the crayon when he's coloring by providing him with a crayon that has been broken in half. The smaller size requires him to use only his thumb and fingers to color, strengthening the small muscles in the hand that are so important for future handwriting skills.

Learning to Write

There are developmental steps involved in early writing, with the first being random scribbling. Next, the child scribbles and makes marks on the paper to express his thoughts, and he may even talk to himself as he works. Even though the completed drawing may not be recognizable to an adult, to your child it makes sense, and he can tell you about his creation. Finally, there will be a transition to symbols with meaning, such as lines and basic shapes.

Activity 3: Felt Board Dressing Fun

Take a medium-sized cardboard cereal box and cover one side of it with a thin layer of glue along the perimeter. Secure a piece of white felt on the side of the box covered with the glue. Allow plenty of time for the glue to dry. While you are waiting, draw the template of a person on a piece of felt. Create various pieces of clothing to fit the felt person, such as a bathing suit, a coat, a sweater, underwear, pants, skirts, tops, shoes, and mittens. Your child will enjoy dressing the "person" for different scenarios. This will provide a wonderful opportunity to discuss dressing appropriately for different types of weather.

Activity 4: Roly Poly

Show your child how to roll a handful of Play-Doh into a hot dog shape. Have him pinch off a small piece and use the tips of his thumb, index finger, and middle finger to make several balls. Encourage him to keep working so that they are as smooth and round as possible. If necessary, remind him to keep the ring and pinkie fingers tucked inside his palm. (Make sure to keep a watchful eye on your child so he does not put any Play-Doh in his mouth).

Dressing Tip

Here is a creative way to teach your toddler to put his coat on. Place the coat backwards on the back of a child-sized chair with the inside of the garment facing outward. Show your child how to stand with his back to the coat and place his arms through the sleeves. As he stands up, he should move the coat over his shoulders. Voilà! The coat is on!

Activity 5: Button Caterpillar

Buttoning and unbuttoning can be a challenging skill to learn, but this buttoning caterpillar will make it fun! You will need one large button, a ribbon that is 6 inches in length, several colors of thick felt, and a permanent marker. Sew a square piece of felt on one end of the ribbon and the button to the other end. Draw two small eyes on the button. Cut out 5 or 6 small felt circles in various colors. Each circle should be large enough to contain a

buttonhole. Cut a small slit in the center of the circles that will permit the button to fit through. Show your toddler how to make a caterpillar by placing the buttons through the holes. Be sure to talk about the different colors as he carries out the activity.

Mary Had a Little Lamb

Mary had a little lamb, little lamb, little lamb,
Mary had a little lamb, its fleece was white as snow.

And everywhere that Mary went, Mary went, Mary went,
And everywhere that Mary went, the lamb was sure to go.

It followed her to school one day,
school one day, school one day,
It followed her to school one day,
which was against the rules.

It made the children laugh and play,
laugh and play, laugh and play,
It made the children laugh and play
to see a lamb at school.

And so the teacher turned it out, turned it out, turned it out,
And so the teacher turned it out, but still it lingered near.

And waited patiently about, patiently about, patiently about,
And waited patiently about till Mary did appear.

"Why does the lamb love Mary so? love Mary so?
love Mary so?
"Why does the lamb love Mary so?" the eager children cry.

"Why, Mary loves the lamb, you know,
the lamb, you know, the lamb, you know,
"Why, Mary loves the lamb, you know,"
the teacher did reply.

Developing Skill: Briefly Stands on One Foot

Balance is an important part of motor skill development, and it is foundational for basic skills such as standing and walking. Balance is also required for more complex skills, such as standing on one foot and kicking a ball. The following activities are great ways for your child to improve his balance.

Activities to Improve Balance

Activity 1: Power Kick

Place 2 empty soda bottles approximately 4 feet apart on the floor. Your child may enjoy decorating them with paint or stickers first. Show your child how to kick a large ball through the "goal." A beach ball will work well. This activity can be made more challenging by bringing the bottles closer together, by using smaller balls, or by stepping farther away from the goal.

Activity 2: Play That Funky Music

Dancing is a fun way to exercise *gross motor skills,* including balance. All you need is some toddler-friendly music. Turn on the tunes and ask your child to join you in a dance. As soon as he hears the music, he will likely start dancing. Once he starts moving to the rhythm, encourage him to imitate a variety of movements, such as swaying, hopping, jumping, and spinning. Be silly and goofy, and have fun as you boogie down together!

Activity 3: Traffic Light Fun

Cut 1 large circle out of construction paper in each of the following colors: red, yellow, and green. The rules of this game are for your toddler to actively move around when you hold up the green circle, move in slow motion when you hold up the yellow circle, and freeze when you hold up the red circle. Explain that this is how a traffic light works. This will surely promote an interesting discussion the next time you approach a traffic light when traveling in the car.

Activity 4: Heads Up!

Place a beanbag on your toddler's head and ask him to walk around the room while keeping the bag balanced on his head. Encourage him to start slowly and then to gradually increase his speed. He can also attempt to keep the beanbag balanced while swaying from side to side and front to back. This activity is sure to elicit a few giggles.

Activity 5: Stepping Stone Adventure

Place a variety of items of different heights on the floor for your child to walk on, such as heavy books. Choose items that are safe to step on and won't allow your child to slip and fall. Show your little one how to walk across the "stepping stones" without touching the floor. This is an adventurous way to develop his balance and coordination.

Developing Skill: Recognizes Colors

Recognizing colors is an important skill that takes time to master. Toddlers learn colors in a fairly sequential developmental process. This process includes matching, recognizing, pointing out, and naming colors. Once your child knows his colors, he can use them to describe the world around him. You can help your little one learn colors by talking about the different colors of items in their immediate surroundings.

Activities for Recognizing Colors

Activity 1: Matching

Paint swatch samples from the hardware store are perfect for a do-it-yourself color-matching activity! Select 4 basic colors, such as red, blue, yellow, and green. You will need 2 samples of each color. Spread the cards out on the table and encourage your child to match the cards while naming the colors. Once he gets the hang of it, turn over several of the cards and play a color-matching memory game. Have fun!

Activity 2: Color Day

Pick a particular color and make that color the focus for the day. For example, Monday might be "Red Day." Have your toddler select red clothing to wear, eat a red apple at snack time, and point out all the red stop signs when riding in the car. Rotate through various colors each day of the week.

Activity 3: Box With Targets

Cut 4 holes in a large box and use magic markers to outline the holes in red, blue, yellow, and green. This will serve as your target. You will also need 3 or 4 beanbags for this activity. Make the bags by sewing 2 squares of colorful fabric together, then fill the bags with beans or rice. Instruct your child to throw the beanbags at the different-colored targets. He will have fun playing the game, and he will also be learning his colors!

Activity 4: Muffin Tin Fun

For this activity, you will need an old 8-cup muffin tin and 8 plastic Easter eggs, 2 each of 4 colors. Fill the top row by placing an egg of each color in the cups and show your child how to match the pattern by putting the matching colored eggs in the empty row below. Encourage him to name the colors as he carries out the activity, and once he masters matching the pattern, have him create a pattern for you to copy. This is an entertaining activity that is good for concentration and eye-hand coordination.

Truth Be Told

Researchers investigated young children's preferences for interior colors of childcare centers and found that red was the preferred color.[91]

London Bridge

London Bridge is falling down,
Falling down, falling down.
London Bridge is falling down,
My fair lady.

Take a key and lock her up,
Lock her up, lock her up.
Take a key and lock her up,
My fair lady.

Scissors Skill Development

Cutting with scissors is a challenging task that takes a considerable amount of practice and requires hand strength and coordination. When your toddler begins to use safe child-sized scissors, make sure that he is holding them correctly with his thumb facing upward. He will begin by making single snips. Offer straws or index cards cut into narrow strips during the snipping stage. When he begins to snip sequentially, avoid giving him flimsy paper to cut. Rather, start with thicker options, such as index cards or card stock, which are much easier to cut.

Developing Skill: Understands Prepositions Such as "on," "in," and "under"

During this age range, your toddler is beginning to understand the meaning of *prepositions*. *Prepositions* are important because they connect parts of a sentence and let us know how one thing relates to another in space. Your child learns these naturally during conversation, but you can make the learning process easier for him with the following activities.

Activities for Teaching Prepositions

Activity 1: Preposition Craft

Here is a fun craft project that is great for learning *prepositions*. You will need the following items: glue, a piece of paper, a 6-inch piece of yarn, a large colorful sticker, a strip of tape, and small and large circles cut out of construction paper. Give your child some basic directions, such as "Glue the small circle in the middle of the paper, and place the sticker under the circle." Once he follows those directions, tell him, "Use the tape to attach the piece of string to the paper directly above the small circle, and glue the large circle beside the string." This is a fun way for your toddler to practice following directions while also learning *prepositions!*

Activity 2: Experiencing Prepositions

Playing on a playground is a fun way for your child to actually experience the meaning of *prepositions*. While he is exploring, talk about what he's doing. For example, "You are sliding under the tunnel, climbing over the bars, walking on a balance beam, and going inside the playhouse." Now it's his turn to describe what he's doing!

Activity 3: In, Over, Under, Beside

Remember the felt board you made in the Activities for Dressing Skills section? You can use that as a playful *preposition* activity. Cut out a variety of felt pieces in different shapes, sizes, and colors, then share a description with your child and ask him to create it. First, tell him to put a circle in the middle of the board. Then have him place other shapes under, over, beside, and on top of the various pieces. He will enjoy the game while reinforcing his understanding of shapes.

Activity 4: Touch-and-Feel Board

Help your toddler make a touch-and-feel board by gluing items such as sandpaper, felt, cotton, and fabrics of different textures onto a sturdy piece of poster board. Tell him what to feel by using *prepositions:* "Touch the soft cotton in the middle of the board. Feel the scratchy sandpaper that is beside the cotton. Is the silky piece of fabric over or under the sandpaper?"

Activity 5: Preposition Review

Reading to your toddler provides the perfect opportunity to review *prepositions.* Point to different parts of an illustration in the book and ask, "Where is the dog?" If your

child has difficulty naming the location, you may want to give him a prompt: "Is the dog under the table or beside the table?" Allow your little one to turn the pages and encourage him to point to pictures to encourage finger isolation.

Epilogue

Epilogue

The toddler years are a whirlwind, with your child gaining new skills every passing day. From learning about boundaries to developing an identity, your child's development is something you have the privilege of witnessing first hand. By being proactive and reading this book, you have learned that you can positively influence your child's development by providing a myriad of learning opportunities on a regular basis. Remember, your child learns through play!

Because your toddler's speech and language skills are constantly expanding, sing to her and read to her frequently. You can use the song lyrics and nursery rhymes included in this book or visit your local library or look online to find others. As her vocabulary grows, your child will be better able to communicate, which will make managing her feelings less challenging—and, ideally, this will lead to fewer temper tantrums.

Toddlers are easily captivated by electronic toys and screens, but you now know that technology is likely to limit parent-child interaction, which will likely hinder learning and language development. With this knowledge,

you won't fall prey to marketers' claims that smartphones, tablets, screen time, and high-tech toys are
beneficial for your toddler's learning because you know
that research does not back such claims. Now that you
know how screen time and digital media use can negatively affect early childhood development, take advantage
of the American Academy of Pediatrics recommendations
for children's media use and let this valuable resource
guide you when making decisions about your child's
technology exposure. It will be especially important to
continue to refer to these recommendations as your
child becomes of school age and moves toward the
preteen and teen years.

As your toddler becomes more proficient with her *gross
motor* and *fine motor skills,* remember to provide her with
plenty of opportunities to be physically active, indoors
and outdoors. Make a point not to let your child shy away
from challenges. Instead, teach her to persevere when the
going gets tough. She will learn that struggles can be
learning opportunities, which will make her grittier! And
when she is successful with a task, remember to praise
her for effort and not intelligence so that she will develop
a *growth mindset.* Finally, when time allows, use the
activities provided in this book to promote your toddler's
physical, cognitive, and social development. Monitor her
developmental milestones, and if you have any concerns,
speak to your pediatrician.

As parents, we want to raise our children well and set
them up for lifelong success, but during the toddler years,
toilet training, temper tantrums, and tears can be overwhelming, to say the least. During stressful times, it is
important to stay calm and do your best to keep a positive
outlook. Take care of yourself by eating well, exercising,
and getting enough sleep. When you are facing a stressful

situation with your toddler, take a deep breath and stay in the moment. Being present is called "mindfulness," and it can help you get through the challenging days. You can even use the "Breathe In, Breathe Out" technique provided in Chapter 3 to relieve stress. Finally, the old saying "It takes a village to raise a child" is true, so don't hesitate to call on your support systems when you are feeling overwhelmed or just need some reinforcement.

It is my hope that this book has provided you with information and tools that will help you navigate the toddler years, which can be challenging as well as magical. No matter what, enjoy spending time with your child, make special memories, and take advantage of every precious moment!

References

1. Weisleder A, Fernald A. Talking to children matters: early language experience strengthens processing and builds vocabulary. *Psychol Sci.* 2013;24(11):2143–2152
2. Diamond A. Activities and programs that improve children's executive functions. *Curr Dir Psychol Sci.* 2012;21(5):335–341
3. Deckner DF, Adamson LB, Bakeman R. Child and maternal contributions to shared reading: effects on language and literacy development. *J Appl Dev Psychol.* 2007;27(1):31–41
4. American Academy of Pediatrics Council on Early Childhood. Literacy promotion: an essential component of primary care pediatric practice. *Pediatrics.* 2014;134(2):404–409
5. Weigel DJ, Martin SS, Bennett KK. Contributions of the home literacy environment to preschool-aged children's emerging literacy and language skills. *Early Child Dev Care.* 2006;176(3-4): 357–378
6. Chen P, Rea C, Shaw R, Bottino CJ. Associations between public library use and reading aloud among families with young children. *J Pediatr.* 2016;173(suppl):221–227
7. Lockwood PL, Seara-Cardoso A, Viding E. Emotion regulation moderates the association between empathy and prosocial behavior. *PLoS One.* 2014;9(5):e96555
8. Becker DR, Maio A, Duncan R, McClelland MM. Behavioral self-regulation and executive function both predict visuomotor skills and early academic achievement. *Early Child Res Q.* 2016;29(4): 411–424
9. Endenburg N, van Lith HA. The influence of animals on the development of children. *Vet J.* 2011;190(2):208–214
10. Keen R. The development of problem solving in young children: a critical cognitive skill. *Annu Rev Psychol.* 2011;62:1–21
11. Iverson JM. Developing language in a developing body: the relationship between motor development and language development. *J Child Lang.* 2010;37(2):229–261
12. Goldfield GS, Harvey A, Grattan K, Adamo KB. Physical activity promotion in the preschool years: a critical period to intervene. *Int J Environ Res Public Health.* 2012;9(4):1326–1342
13. Fuemmeler BF, Anderson CB, Mâsse LC. Parent-child relationship of directly measured physical activity. *Int J Behav Nutr Phys Act.* 2011;8:17
14. Grissmer D, Grimm KJ, Aiyer SM, Murrah WM, Steele JS. Fine motor skills and early comprehension of the world: two new school readiness indicators. *Dev Psychol.* 2010;46(5):1008–1017

15. MacDonald M, Lipscomb S, McClelland MM, et al. Relations of preschoolers' visual-motor and object manipulation skills with executive function and social behavior. *Res Q Exerc Sport.* 2016;87(4):396–407

16. Cameron CE, Brock LL, Murrah WM, et al. Fine motor skills and executive function both contribute to kindergarten achievement. *Child Dev.* 2012;83(4):1229–1244

17. Luyckx K, Tildesley EA, Soenens B, et al. Parenting and trajectories of children's maladaptive behaviors: a 12-year prospective community study. *J Clin Child Adolesc Psychol.* 2011;40(3):468–478

18. Piotrowski JT, Lapierre MA, Linebarger DL. Investigating correlates of self-regulation in early childhood with a representative sample of English-speaking American families. *J Child Fam Stud.* 2013;22(3):423–436

19. Milevsky A, Schlechter M, Netter S, Keehn D. Maternal and paternal parenting styles in adolescents: associations with self-esteem, depression and life-satisfaction. *J Child Fam Stud.* 2007;16(1):39–47

20. American Academy of Pediatrics. Discipline. American Academy of Pediatrics Web site. https://www.aap.org/en-us/about-the-aap/aap-press-room/aap-press-room-media-center/pages/discipline.aspx. Accessed August 31, 2017

21. Simons LG, Conger RD. Linking mother-father differences in parenting to a typology of family parenting styles and adolescent outcomes. *J Fam Issues.* 2007;28(2):212–241

22. Rinaldi CM, Howe N. Mothers' and fathers' parenting styles and associations with toddlers' externalizing, internalizing, and adaptive behaviors. *Early Child Res Q.* 2012;27(2):266–273

23. Gunderson EA, Gripshover SJ, Romero C, Dweck CS, Goldin-Meadow S, Levine SC. Parent praise to 1- to 3-year-olds predicts children's motivational frameworks 5 years later. *Child Dev.* 2013;84(5):1526–1541

24. Mueller CM, Dweck CS. Praise for intelligence can undermine children's motivation and performance. *J Pers Soc Psychol.* 1998;75(1):33–52

25. Duckworth AL, Peterson C, Matthews MD, Kelly DR. Grit: perseverance and passion for long-term goals. *J Pers Soc Psychol.* 2007;92(6):1087–1101

26. Mischel W, Ebbesen EB, Zeiss AR. Cognitive and attentional mechanisms in delay of gratification. *J Pers Soc Psychol.* 1972;21(2):204–218

27. Steelandt S, Thierry B, Broihanne MH, Dufour V. The ability of children to delay gratification in an exchange task. *Cognition.* 2012;122(3):416–425

28. Casey BJ, Somerville LH, Gotlib IH, et al. Behavioral and neural correlates of delay of gratification 40 years later. *Proc Natl Acad Sci U S A.* 2011;108(36):14998–15003

29. O'Connor C, Stagnitti K. Play, behavior, language and social skills: the comparison of a play and non-play intervention within a specialist school setting. *Res Dev Disabil.* 2011;32(3): 1205–1211

30. He M, Xiang F, Zeng Y, et al. Effect of time spent outdoors at school on the development of myopia among children in China: a randomized clinical trial. *JAMA.* 2015;314(11): 1142–1148

31. Aggio D, Smith L, Fisher A, Hamer M. Mothers' perceived proximity to green space is associated with TV viewing time in children: the Growing Up in Scotland study. *Prev Med.* 2015;70: 46–49

32. Dadvand P, Nieuwenhuijsen MJ, Esnaola M, et al. Green spaces and cognitive development in primary schoolchildren. *Proc Natl Acad Sci U S A.* 2015;112(26):7937–7942

33. Flouri E, Midouhas E, Joshi H. The role of urban neighbourhood green space in children's emotional and behavioral resilience. *J Environ Psychol.* 2014;40:179–186

34. Berman MG, Jonides J, Kaplan S. The cognitive benefits of interacting with nature. *Psychol Sci.* 2008;19(12):1207–1212

35. Levine SC, Ratliff KR, Huttenlocher J, Cannon J. Early puzzle play: a predictor of preschoolers' spatial transformation skill. *Dev Psychol.* 2012;48(2):530–542

36. Morrissey A-M, Brown PM. Mother and toddler activity in the Zone of Proximal Development for pretend play as a predictor of higher child IQ. *Gift Child Q.* 2009;53(2):106–120

37. Howard-Jones P, Taylor J, Sutton L. The effect of play on the creativity of young children during subsequent activity. *Early Child Dev Care.* 2002;172(4):323–328

38. Ebert M, Hoffman JD, Ivcevic I, Phan C, Brackets MA. Teaching emotion and creativity skills though art: a workshop for children. *Int J Creativity Problem Solving.* 2015;25(2):23–35

39. Brownell CA, Svetlova M, Nichols S. To share or not to share: when do toddlers respond to another's needs? *Infancy.* 2009;14(1):117–130

40. Fisher K, Hirsh-Pasek K, Golinkoff RM, Singer DG, Berk L. Playing around in school: implications for learning and educational policy. In: Nathan P, Pellegrini AD, eds. *Oxford Handbook of the Development of Play*. Oxford, England: Oxford University Press; 2010:341–360

41. Brown A, Shifrin D, Hill D. Beyond "turn it off": how to advise families on media use. *AAP News*. 2015;36(10):1–3

42. Rideout V. *Zero to Eight: Children's Media Use in America 2013*. San Francisco, CA: Common Sense Media; 2013

43. Zimmerman FJ, Christakis DA, Meltzoff AN. Television and DVD/video viewing in children younger than 2 years. *Arch Pediatr Adolesc Med*. 2007;161(5):473–479

44. Fitzpatrick C, Barnett T, Pagani LS. Early exposure to media violence and later child adjustment. *J Dev Behav Pediatr*. 2012;33(4):291–297

45. Wartella E, Hideout V, Lauricella A, Connell S. *Parenting in the Age of Digital Technology: A National Survey. Report of the Center on Media and Human Development, School of Communication, Northwestern University*. Evanston, IL: Northwestern University; 2013

46. Barr R, Lauricella A, Zack E, Calvert SL. Infant and early childhood exposure to adult-directed and child-directed television programming: relations with cognitive skills at age four. *Merrill-Palmer Q*. 2010;56(1):21–48

47. Tomopoulos S, Dreyer BP, Berkule S, Fierman AH, Brockmeyer C, Mendelsohn A. Infant media exposure and toddler development. *Arch Pediatr Adolesc Med*. 2010;164(12):1105–1111

48. American Academy of Pediatrics. American Academy of Pediatrics announces new recommendations for children's media use. American Academy of Pediatrics Web site. https://www.aap.org/en-us/about-the-aap/aap-press-room/Pages/American-Academy-of-Pediatrics-Announces-New-Recommendations-for-Childrens-Media-Use.aspx. Updated October 21, 2016. Accessed August 31, 2017

49. Strouse GA, O'Doherty K, Troseth GL. Effective coviewing: preschoolers' learning from video after a dialogic questioning intervention. *Dev Psychol*. 2013;49(12):2368–2382

50. Kabali HK, Irigoyen MM, Nunez-Davis R, et al. Exposure and use of mobile media devices by young children. *Pediatrics*. 2015;136(6):1044–1050

51. Lapierre MA, Piotrowski JT, Linebarger DL. Background television in the homes of US children. *Pediatrics*. 2012;130(5):839–846

52. Kirkorian HL, Pempek TA, Murphy LA, Schmidt ME, Anderson DR. The impact of background television on parent-child interaction. *Child Dev.* 2009;80(5):1350–1359

53. Christakis DA, Gilkerson J, Richards JA, et al. Audible television and decreased adult words, infant vocalizations, and conversational turns: a population-based study. *Arch Pediatr Adolesc Med.* 2009;163(6):554–558

54. Hart B, Risley TR. *Meaningful Differences in the Everyday Experiences of Young American Children.* Baltimore, MD: Paul H. Brookes; 1995

55. Courage ML, Murphy AN, Goulding S, Setliff AE. When the television is on: the impact of infant-directed video on 6- and 18-month-olds' attention during toy play and on parent-infant interaction. *Infant Behav Dev.* 2010;33(2):176–188

56. Tomopoulos S, Cates CB, Dreyer BP, Fierman AH, Berkule SB, Mendelsohn AL. Children under the age of two are more likely to watch inappropriate background media than older children. *Acta Paediatr.* 2014;103(5):546–552

57. Hirsh-Pasek K, Zosh JM, Golinkoff RM, Gray JH, Robb MB, Kaufman J. Putting education in "educational" apps: lessons from the science of learning. *Psychol Sci Public Interest.* 2015;16(1):3–34

58. Ahearne C, Dilworth S, Rollings R, Livingstone V, Murray D. Touch-screen technology usage in toddlers. *Arch Dis Child.* 2016;101(2):181–183

59. Chiong C, Shuler C. *Learning: Is There an App for That? Investigations of Young Children's Usage and Learning With Mobile Devices and Apps.* New York, NY: The Joan Ganz Cooney Center at Sesame Workshop; 2010

60. Chassiakos YR, Radesky J, Christakis D, Moreno MA, Cross C; American Academy of Pediatrics Council on Communications and Media. Children and adolescents and digital media. *Pediatrics.* 2016;138(5):e20162593

61. Sosa AV. Association of the type of toy used during play with the quantity and quality of parent-infant communication. *JAMA Pediatr.* 2016;170(2):132–137

62. Garrison MM, Liekweg K, Christakis DA. Media use and child sleep: the impact of content, timing, and environment. *Pediatrics.* 2011;128(1):29–35

63. Jackson DM, Djafarian K, Stewart J, Speakman JR. Increased television viewing is associated with elevated body fatness but not with lower total energy expenditure in children. *Am J Clin Nutr.* 2009;89(4):1031–1036

64. Certain LK, Kahn RS. Prevalence, correlates, and trajectory of television viewing among infants and toddlers. *Pediatrics.* 2002;109(4):634–642

65. Roseberry S, Hirsh-Pasek K, Golinkoff RM. Skype me! Socially contingent interactions help toddlers learn language. *Child Dev.* 2014;85(3):956–970

66. Schmidt ME, Pempek TA, Kirkorian HL, Lund AF, Anderson DR. The effects of background television on the toy play behavior of very young children. *Child Dev.* 2008;79(4):1137–1151

67. Christakis DA, Zimmerman FJ. Early television viewing is associated with protesting turning off the television at age 6. *MedGenMed.* 2006;8(2):63

68. American Academy of Pediatrics. Toddler. HealthyChildren.org Web site. https://www.healthychildren.org/english/ages-stages/toddler/pages/default.aspx. Accessed August 31, 2017

69. Centers for Disease Control and Prevention. Developmental milestones. Learn the Signs—Act Early Web site. https://www.cdc.gov/ncbddd/actearly/milestones/index.html. Accessed August 31, 2017

70. Pavličikovà D. Laterality. Early Education Web site. http://www.schola-europaea.eu/ELC/popups/21.pdf. Accessed August 31, 2017

71. Dawson G, Bernier R. A quarter century of progress on the early detection and treatment of autism spectrum disorder. *Dev Psychopathol.* 2013;25(4 Pt 2):1455–1472

72. American Academy of Pediatrics. What are the early signs of autism? HealthyChildren.org Web site. https://www.healthychildren.org/English/health-issues/conditions/Autism/Pages/Early-Signs-of-Autism-Spectrum-Disorders.aspx. Updated September 4, 2015. Accessed August 31, 2017

73. Flom R, Pick AD. Verbal encouragement and joint attention in 18-month-old infants. *Infant Behav Dev.* 2003;26(2):121–134

74. Cartmill EA, Armstrong BF III, Gleitman LR, Goldin-Meadow S, Medina TN, Trueswell JC. Quality of early parent input predicts child vocabulary 3 years later. *Proc Natl Acad Sci U S A.* 2013;110(28):11278–11283

75. Centers for Disease Control and Prevention. Using time-out. Essentials for Parenting Toddlers and Preschoolers Web site. https://www.cdc.gov/parents/essentials/timeout/index.html. Updated August 24, 2016. Accessed August 31, 2017

76. Repacholi BM, Gopnik A. Early reasoning about desires: evidence from 14- and 18-month-olds. *Dev Psychol.* 1997;33(1):12–21

77. Nakagawa M, Ohta H, Nagaoki Y, et al. Daytime nap controls toddlers' nighttime sleep. *Sci Rep.* 2016;6:27246

78. American Academy of Pediatrics. Healthy sleep habits: how many hours does your child need? HealthyChildren.org Web site. https://www.healthychildren.org/English/healthy-living/sleep/Pages/Healthy-Sleep-Habits-How-Many-Hours-Does-Your-Child-Need.aspx. Updated March 23, 2017. Accessed August 31, 2017

79. Jana LA, Shu J. *Food Fights: Winning the Nutritional Challenges of Parenthood Armed With Insight, Humor, and a Bottle of Ketchup.* 2nd ed. Elk Grove Village, IL: American Academy of Pediatrics; 2012

80. American Academy of Pediatrics. How to buy safe toys. HealthyChildren.org Web site. https://www.healthychildren.org/English/safety-prevention/at-home/Pages/How-to-Buy-Safe-Toys.aspx. Updated December 2, 2016. Accessed August 31, 2017

81. Amsterdam B. Mirror self-image reactions before age two. *Dev Psychobiol.* 1972;5(4):297–305

82. Brownell CA, Zerwas S, Ramani GB. "So big": The development of body self-awareness in toddlers. *Child Dev.* 2007;78(5):1426–1440

83. Massaro DW. Multiple influences on vocabulary acquisition: parental input dominates. In: Proceedings from Interspeech 2016; September 8–12, 2016; San Francisco, CA:878–882

84. Sarkadi A, Kristiansson R, Oberklaid F, Bremberg S. Fathers' involvement and children's developmental outcomes: a systematic review of longitudinal studies. *Acta Paediatr.* 2008;97(2):153–158

85. Morgan A, Nutbrown C, Hannon P. Fathers' involvement in young children's literacy development: implications for family literacy programmes. *Br Educ Res J.* 2009;35(2):167–185

86. Green JA,Whitney PG, Potegal M. Screaming, yelling, whining, and crying: categorical and intensity differences in vocal expressions of anger and sadness in children's tantrums. *Emotion.* 2011;11(5):1124–1133

87. Wansink B, Just DR, Payne CR, Klinger MZ. Attractive names sustain increased vegetable intake in schools. *Prev Med.* 2012;55(4):330–332

88. Brownell CA, Svetlova M, Anderson R, Nichols S, Drummond J. Socialization of early prosocial behavior: parents' talk about emotions is associated with sharing and helping in toddlers. *Infancy.* 2013;18:91–119

89. Milteer RM, Ginsburg KR, Mulligan DA; American Academy of Pediatrics Council on Communications and Media and Committee on Psychosocial Aspects of Child and Family Health. The importance of play in promoting healthy child development and maintaining strong parent-child bond: focus on children in poverty. *Pediatrics.* 2012;129(1):e204–e213

90. Manners-Jones DE, Greenberg M, Crowley M. Early social-emotional functioning and public health: the relationship between kindergarten and social competence and future wellness. *Am J Public Health.* 2015;105(1):2283–2290

91. Read MA, Upington D. Young children's color preferences in the interior environment. *Early Child Education J.* 2009;36(6): 491–496

Glossary

Asymmetrical bilateral integration: Each side of the body carries out a different action or movement to complete a single task (for example, tying shoes).

Authoritarian parenting style: A structured approach to parenting that involves setting firm rules and the expectation that those rules will be followed without discussion or question.

Authoritative parenting style: A responsive approach to parenting that involves having high standards and setting boundaries and allows for discussion between parents and children related to rules and consequences.

Bilateral skills: The ability to use the right and left sides of the body together to carry out actions (for example, shaking a toy while holding it with both hands).

Constructive play: Organized and goal-directed play that involves building and creating.

Critical period (also called "sensitive period"): A time frame during the life span in which a specific developmental stage usually occurs.

Dexterity: The ability to synchronize movements with the hands, the body, or both.

Executive functions: A set of mental skills that mediate attention, focusing, remembering, and planning.

Fine motor skills: The ability to coordinate the hands and fingers when manipulating small objects.

Fixed mindset: The belief that one's intelligence and talents are unchanging.

Grit: Consistently demonstrating passion and perseverance to achieve long-term goals.

Gross motor skills: The ability to control the large muscle groups of the body to carry out activities such as standing, walking, jumping, and climbing.

Growth mindset: The belief that one's abilities can be developed by practicing and working hard.

Joint attention: Two individuals sharing their focus on an object or person.

Midline: The imaginary vertical plane that divides the left and right halves of the body.

Nesting: When one object fits snugly inside the other.

Object permanence: The awareness that an object exists even when the item is out of sight.

Parallel play: When a child plays independently alongside others with limited interaction taking place.

Permissive parenting style: An affirmative and highly responsive approach to parenting that is nonpunitive and involves avoiding conflict and confrontation.

Physical play: Play that involves movement and exercise.

Pincer grasp: The use of the thumb and index finger to pick up a small object.

Preposition: A function word that describes the position of one thing relative to another.

Pretend or symbolic play: Involves role-play, dramatization, and use of the imagination.

Pronated grasp: Holding an object or writing utensil with the palm facing down.

Proprioception: The unconscious awareness of body position.

Reciprocal bilateral integration: Moving the right and left sides of the body in opposite directions (for example, crawling).

Self-control: The ability to control one's emotions, impulses, and actions.

Social play (also called "cooperative play"): Play that involves working together with others to achieve a shared goal.

Solitary play: When a child plays alone with no attention to others.

Symmetrical bilateral integration: Use of the right and left sides of the body in which one side of the body mirrors the actions of the other side.

Uninvolved parenting style (also called "disengaged parenting style"): An approach to parenting in which parents are unresponsive, indifferent, and uninvolved.

Visual acuity: Sharpness or clarity of vision.

Visual discrimination: Awareness of the distinct features of an item or the ability to see slight differences between objects or pictures.

Visual perceptual skills: The skill of organizing the information that the eyes take in and making sense of that information.

Index

A